# GLYNN BOYD HARTE'S VENICE

# Glynn Boyd Harte's

# VENICE

## HAMISH HAMILTON
### LONDON

HAMISH HAMILTON LTD

Published by the Penguin Group
27 Wrights Lane, London W8 5TZ, England
Viking Penguin Inc, 40 West 23rd Street, New York, New York 10010, U.S.A.
Penguin Books Australia Ltd, Ringwood, Victoria, Australia
Penguin Books Canada Ltd, 2801 John Street, Markham, Ontario, Canada L3R 1B4
Penguin Books (N.Z.) Ltd, 182–190 Wairau Road, Auckland 10, New Zealand

Penguin Books Ltd, Registered Offices: Harmondsworth, Middlesex, England

First published in Great Britain 1988 by
Hamish Hamilton Ltd

Copyright © 1988 by Hamish Hamilton Ltd

1 3 5 7 9 10 8 6 4 2

British Library Cataloguing in Publication Data

Boyd-Harte, Glynn
Venice.
1. Italian visual arts. Venetian visual
arts
I. Title
709′.45′31

ISBN 0–241–12428–X

Printed in Spain by Cayfosa Industria Gráfica, Barcelona.

To the memory of
BRIAN ROBB
1913–1979
and
COLIN McMORDIE
1948–1985

ADRIAN ordered another bottle. Above us wild swoops of naked gilded ladies extravagantly gestured to the delights vividly painted on the ceiling, the Joys of Travel saturated with the vivid blue of the Mediterranean. Azure and gold – the South beckoned.

Dinner had been excellent: waiters with aprons to the ground glided through belle époque luxury bringing us plates of delicate pink cold lamb ringed by mounds of quivering aspic. Adrian had recently chosen to paint and draw abroad for a year – according to him for tax-reasons – and we were having a very jolly, gossipy reunion. From our table in the warm, sumptuous restaurant we were able to look down into the nearly empty railway station below. It was late, but our train was there waiting. Out of the vast gloom wiggled a silent caterpillar of baggage. We recognized ours – my portfolio, sketching stool, paints, a large leather case containing all Carrie's frocks – and saw it safely loaded onto the right train. We sipped our wine, sinking back satiated and complacent. This was the way to travel. We did not realize we would never see that luggage again.

Moments before the train was due to leave, and the bottle empty, Adrian and his assistant helped us onto the train. I think we were already asleep as we left Paris, slowly pulling out of the Gare de Lyon, leaving the last waiter possibly whistling as the Train Bleu closed.

In the past you had vaguely to bribe the sleeping-car attendant to prevent all the various border guards from awakening you at regular intervals and demanding documents. This no longer seems to happen, but we were only to discover the next day that all the couplings and uncouplings occurring through the night were mainly confined to the luggage compartments.

Carrie, tiresomely, refuses to fly – a method of transport which I rather enjoy – so this time we had to chug (or whatever trains do these days) through the Alps. There is, I must admit, the excitement and beauty of drawing the blind at dawn to look up to the pale pink summits of snow. I prefer (sipping a cocktail) to look down on them peeping above the clouds. But there is the huge and symbolic advantage of going through the tunnel and emerging into the great moving surge of light that is Italy.

Little thimbles of potent espresso coffee are handed in through the window from the platform at Domodossola. Soon one can see warm red pantiled roofs offset by the blue of Lake Como. There are rapid and tantalizing glimpses of that enchanted isle, Isola Bella, with its palace, follies and curious grottoes set about by strutting peacocks (these have to be imagined as you speed past).

Stopping at Milan, its approach very similar to that of Manchester, gives you just time to marvel at the extraordinary megalomaniac nature of the station. I am happy to pace its Metro-Goldwyn-Mayer Marble Halls with their endless escalators, bronze uplighters and chunky stripped-neo-classical details. You feel it was made more for chariots than trains, and if it had been built in England it would have been demolished years ago.

The same train becomes distinctly more local as we proceed across the flat plain. Somehow it is now filled with an inexplicable mixture of soldiers, housewives, distinguished ladies in fur coats with their grandchildren, and students with backpacks. They all babble utterly incomprehensively.

As you begin to approach Venice (you reading Augustus J. C. Hare's guidebook, everyone else eating salami), excitement mounts. Villages begin to sprout thin campaniles based more and more on *the* Campanile. Almost imperceptibly, you are gradually surrounded by rundown tenements, high-rise flats, oil refineries, smoking industrial complexes, motorway interchanges and huge advertisements for Fiat, Peroni, Campari. Everyone gets out as the train stops at Mestre; we are alone at last and almost there.

Many books tell you not to look out of the window when crossing the narrow embankment that connects the city to the mainland: I disagree – I am always thrilled by a first strained glimpse. The lagoon, as we skim over its surface, is always pale, gentle and timeless.

Lorenzetti, in his incomparable guide *Venice and its Lagoon*, first published in 1926 and translated into memorably period prose, describes his sensations on arrival at the station: 'Leaving behind the noisy turmoil that always accompanies the arrival of a train, stretched comfortably on the cushions of the gondola, we allow ourselves to be carried, lulled by its rhythmic motion, along the Grand Canal, through twisting waterways filled with shadows and sudden silences, wrapt in this peace, with this new enjoyment that, from the first moment, Venice offers to those who come to her to know and to understand her.'

Alas, this was different from our own experience. Although I longed to think I had come to Venice to know and to understand her, we first had to put our minds to the fact that the luggage compartment on our train had utterly disappeared. This involved finding a dingy little office round the back and waiting rather a long time until someone appeared. We struggled with their language. They shrugged at our plight. We were on the wrong train? No, we were on the same train and had seen our luggage loaded in Paris. Possibly the customs had removed the compartment, then, in Domodossola. How could we find out? With extreme reluctance, they telephoned to discover that that had indeed been the case. What could we do? Well, today was Friday, so after that was the weekend, and Monday, of course, was an important National Holiday which meant Tuesday was out, so perhaps if we were to return on either Wednesday or Thursday we could again telephone Domodossola to see if they could release the luggage, which would then take, say, a couple of days to arrive. And there would be the standard handling charge of 95,000 lire.

What are possessions anyway but a lot of old frocks and memories? Pencils, paper and paint could easily be bought in town, indeed the absence of heavy clutter meant we could arrive at the waterdoor of our hotel unimpeded and with panache.

In Reception they did not bat an eyelid at our lack of luggage. I asked if it was usual for guests to have had their luggage officially stolen. Ah yes, they replied, but more usually at the airport. At the station it was rare. Nobody, from the officials at the station to the concierge of the hotel, had regarded this loss as anything other than mundane.

On first waking in Venice the quiet slop of the canal so close still sounds like sleep. Shortly, piecing together where you are in the shuttered blackness, the slop turns to a gloop like a gentle dove's cooing. A nearby bell begins to jangle: a funny hoarse hollow sound like a bell on a lost Alpine cow. It is soon joined by another, further away, horribly cracked and discordant, and another and another until a whole herd of cattle is assembled. Some have called it a Brocade of Bells. If a Pope has happened to die they toll relentlessly. If, on the other hand, a new Pope has been revealed they rejoice and peal, merrily practising scales and trills all day. I have heard both within the space of a week.

All too soon, however, the sounds become louder, threatening, intolerable. In the distance a faint humming turns into a distinct throbbing which turns into a loud insistent pounding as the first motorboat passes under your window. In its wake the gloop slop turns to an angry slap, like that of wet blankets on your face. That is only the start. It is rapidly followed by the refuse-collection boat which sounds exactly like the combination of a jet-engine and a pneumatic drill, all within feet of your face. This is compounded by the unrelenting hearty hails and shouts of the exuberant refuse-collectors. A modern Wagner could make much of their wild, raucous 'Hyee Hyee!' rather than the traditionally melancholy, resigned 'Hoya Hoya!' of the gondoliers when going round corners of canals.

The most inexplicable sound I have heard on waking in Venice occurred more recently and in a different place. I was sharing a small apartment with Edmund, a painter friend, and I was awoken by him next door in the kitchen. He was noisily hitting cube sugar with a rolling-pin to try and reduce it to its granulated state. Although the local shop, only a few yards away, was piled high with bags of the wretched stuff, Edmund stated quite categorically that it was utterly unobtainable in the whole of Venice. Hence he was savagely attacking these poor little cubes with the bluntest of instruments – occasionally with success. From then on, what with the hammering, and shattered sugar ricocheting in all directions, there was no peace.

Gulls shriek and the whole place is throbbing, shouting and pounding. It is the noisiest city in the world and it is time to get up.

I open the shutters and stand transfixed by the view. Downstairs, at breakfast, there is a polite cosmopolitan hum. The Swedish family have two cropped-haired blue-eyed children who simply stare ahead startled, and never say a word. Lucky parents. There is a French couple, very chic; when they talk their eyes never leave each other's faces. There is a plain lady, alone and apart, wearing trousers, observing everyone. I thought she might be a novelist. There is a family of blond Slavs with piggy eyes, and as we pass one table I overhear someone say in English, 'Whatever would Miriam Stoppard say . . .'

Antonio, the waiter, in the tightest of trousers and the thickest of cummerbunds, is utterly charming and greets everyone in their own language, so there is 'God morgon', 'Bon jour', 'Agoodamornink' around the room as he smiles and wiggles off to bring blood-red freshly-squeezed orange juice. He graciously presents a red rose to Carrie. Foaming jugs of milk arrive with coffee and curious, light, delicious, slightly chalky rolls, quite unlike any other bread anywhere. 'Latte o limone?' asks the hotel Lothario.

At the other end of the room by the fan of gladioli, a rather grand elderly English woman in tweeds is teaching Italian to her young tracksuited grandchildren. 'Over here we say GRART-SEA-*AYE* and PEAR FAV-VOR-*AY*. Now say it after me. And today we are goin' to look at the paintin's in the AKA-*DAME*-EYA. Now say after me AKA-*DAME*-EYA . . .'

As we leave the hotel I glance up and see the plain, trousered lady novelist, armed with canvas and paints, has begun her first *esquisse* of the day from her window. Another artist.

In the morning we have decided to wander at random in the city, meet for a picnic lunch, and in the afternoon take a boat over the lagoon to the Lido and on to Torcello, a spaciousness after the maze of the morning. Let us start, though, by doing what I always do on arriving in Venice and walk the short distance to the Zattere and right round the Dogana and back again. But before that – and most important – our first purchase, a tube of toothpaste, Pasta del Capitano, my favourite with its delicious taste of cloves; damn, they've modernized the lettering but luckily it still retains the signed sepia photograph of Dottore Ciccarelli on the pack. How confident and secure he looks with his fine thick upturned moustache, and how like he is to the photograph of someone whose bones we are going to examine later, in the cemetery.

Already down the short canal by San Trovaso we have passed those familiar shops. Ah! their smells, and the smells of Venice! Overlaying a mild bedrock of cats and drains there are great gusts of freshly-ground coffee, new bread, fresh baking of cakes and frying of fish. This last can be smelt for miles and is only marginally more potent than the after-shave of the natives. Add to all this the tang of varnish, lacquer, and newly-carved wood. And there are the marvellous vegetable and flower stalls.

Our spirits soar as we reach the Zattere. Before us glitters the Giudecca canal teeming with all manner of boats, ferries, tugs, barges, tankers, liners and humble vaporetti arriving at the Zattere stop like slow bumblebees. Across the canal we glimpse, shimmering, the domes and curious minaret-like bell towers of the Redentore. Seeing all this I cannot understand why writers, particularly the English, have made Venice such a dismal place, a shabby maze of nostalgia, depression, obsession and melancholy.

Dazzled with so much light and activity we walk for a moment

before plunging into the cool of the Gesuati church. Inside all is spacious calm. It used to be very down at heel and dull, but it is now spectacularly restored. The Tiepolo on the ceiling takes one's breath away. The Madonna on the left wears a variety of seasonal garments. At the moment she is showing off her spring collection. We recall, one Christmas, this church got our Worst Taste Crib Award for a truly spectacular display of astro-turf, rockery and plastic; the infant Christ lying in a nest of shredded cellophane was a Barbie-doll.

Outside again, rounding a bend, crossing a bridge, the magical pink-and-white, domed and towered San Giorgio Maggiore, both floating and soaring, comes into view. We pass the little platform projecting onto the water, where we are to have cocktails this evening. At the Bucintoro Club we notice some boys polishing the upturned bottoms of shiny sleek boats. We think of Baron Corvo.

On top of the huge gilded globe of the Customs House, supported by two bronze Atlases, there is another gilded lady. But, unlike the rather blowsy ladies beckoning us to travel in the Train Bleu the other evening, this is a much more formal affair, severely classical and rather unbending. She is more beautiful than her French sister. She is Fortune and moves with the wind. On such a famously beautiful spot, the Punta della Dogana, all I can do is bring your attention to the tiny inscription on the elaborate iron lamp in front of you. It says:

FONDERIA DI FERRO IN VE. N̲I̲
DI THEODOR E HASSELQUIST ET C̲

This inspired John Sparrow's masterly poem *Santa Maria della Salute*, which ends:

> *When the globe dissolves for me*
> *And the land is lost in sea*
> *When I cross the last lagoon*
> *Starless, and without a moon,*
> *Faithful still beneath the dome*
> *Be they there to light me home*
> *Shining from the farther shore*
> *Hasselquist and Theodor.*

We turn and begin to walk up the side of the Grand Canal. The rustication, heavy grilles and high bold voussoirs around dioclesian windows of this façade of the Customs House have the same sublimity as the Old Newgate Gaol, and are a perfect foil to the riot of Santa Maria della Salute lurking round the corner. What a wonderful moment it is turning into the little paved campo with its simple well to look up to the extravagant white foaming display of domes and scrolls. As at San Marco, the imagery always seems to return to that of the sea. Barnacle-white, its two domes rise like spineless sea-urchins precipitated out of the waves, leaving the large curlicule volutes as petrified froth. In its fantasy, clothing an underlying rationality, it typifies the whole of Venice.

From the bottom of the shallow ample steps as one looks up to the great patinated bronze entrance in the centre, the domes and swirls disappear behind the pediment, and it looks quite a different building, graver, grander even, with remarkable chiaroscuro effects in the bold carving of niches, statues and capitals. We shall be going in later, but now let us pass on over the wooden bridge and under the arch. At the end of the tunnel we retrace our steps: it may seem eccentric in the extreme but I thoroughly recommend this in order to experience the pleasure of walking back through the low, dark tunnel with the bright plain white cliff walls at the end, to emerge once more into the light with an eruption of domes and scrolls before you. I can never decide which is the best approach – to turn a corner or go through a tunnel. Both are glorious so I do both.

Back under the arch, winding our way through narrow brick passages towards the Accademia, we come across the inevitable gaggle of earnest young Americans standing in awe before the ugly glass-encrusted gates of the Guggenheim. If, however, you chance to pass by on a day when entrance to the Museum is free, the gaggle will have turned to a jostling horde. The Museum is housed in the unfinished Palazzo Venier dei Leoni – a huge building which was only completed to the top of the basement storey. To my mind this was quite far enough. The only interest of the gallery is the way in which Mrs Guggenheim actually lived, surrounded by this now very dated-looking modern art; particularly as, these days, people are as interested in interiors as in paintings. In other words, it could have been preserved as a period piece. Instead, the interior has recently all been swept away and every compartment reduced to the bland white box beloved of modernists. It could be anywhere. Much the same has been done to the Ca' d'Oro, as we shall see. Likewise the garden, a rare commodity in Venice, has been paved over, though you might be amused to read the names inscribed in a corner of all Mrs Guggenheim's dogs and daughters buried there.

Shortly, passing the English Church and that secret little trattoria that everyone knows about kept by the three sisters, and the Accademia itself, we are back where we started from. We might have coffee, but do not. We are eager to press on.

Already I have been looking at maps: Venice fanatics love them and I am no exception. I pore over them with pleasure, notice minor differences, plan imaginary routes, commit whole sections to memory, which is just as well since we are aiming to cover the whole city on foot. This would actually take rather more than a morning, but is perfectly possible since it is not a large city and is criss-crossed with a whole variety of calle, strade, rive, fondamente, ruge, salizzade and rami that are the streets of Venice.

Even seen on a map Venice preserves its sea imagery, having the shape of a crustacean, a lobster perhaps, or one of those curious unidentifiable things they find in the lagoon. The Giudecca island certainly looks like a detached claw. Winding like a ribbon or a necklace in an inverted S shape through the middle is the Grand Canal. It is this switchback shape that is the pleasure and pain of topographical artists. I can never work it out. The sun hits it at startling angles just as the Campanile has the disconcerting habit of looming up where one least expects it, and many times I have arrived to paint or draw a particular building only to find the sun has either left it or will take hours to arrive.

The plan does, however, make much more sense if you think of the canals as the main thoroughfares, as of course they used to be. Palaces, almost impossible to find on foot, are simpler to reach by water. The main thoroughfare, the Grand Canal, is barely glimpsed by the pedestrian; indeed it is quite difficult to see it except from the bridges, unless you know the right alleyways. So let us bear in mind we are devoting a whole morning to a slightly unnatural activity – walking. Due to the fascinating and complex way in which the Republic of Venice evolved and developed, there was never one particularly fashionable area. Each of the six sestiers or districts retains a distinct character of its own, and tends to have its own main square, its own particular great church, and a smattering of palaces. Although the Grand Canal is almost completely lined with what today are called palaces, there are other equally grand ones elsewhere. There was even one palace, the megalomaniac Palazzo Pisani, which tried to grow sideways in order to get a Grand Canal façade. This self-aggrandizement was firmly prevented by the State. It still looks a little resentful.

It must be admitted that architecture does peter out in the poorer quarters around the edges, but even these areas have a charm of their own as artists from Lord Leighton to Canaletto have found. Although I do not, of course, care for all the modern housing developments, especially on the newly-created islands, I have curiously become quite fond of the dreaded Piazzale Roma – it is such a bizzare contrast and serves to remind us what the rest of the real world is like. I suppose this is a form of inverted place snobbery, but I naturally gravitate towards the more out-of-the-way areas, the Cannaregio for instance, if only to try to escape from the blight of tourists, particularly when I am working. There are still areas I have not quite got the hang of. But, no matter, let us fold up the map, for one of the pleasures of walking here is getting lost. As in life, there are blind alleys, but unlike life you cannot be lost here for long.

Noting that the new Fellini film is on at the cinema by the Accademia (we might go when it rains) we cross the familiar Rio San Trovaso by the bridge with simple gothic railings. We look down this canal from our corner room in the hotel. Following the shops (liquorice, marrons glacés, books) and going under the arch we come to the Campo San Barnaba. It was here, under the influence of Edward Lear, that I first tasted and liked marsala, but today I think I will have an Americano. You can sit and observe the bushes growing out of the rather dull façade of the church. Delights beckon in all directions. To the right the narrow calle leading down to the vaporetto stop is filled with the smell of varnish and lacquer from the workshops carving rococo frames: to the left on the corner is a spectacular delicatessen selling all manner of deliciousness, and down the calle lunga is a wonderful mixture of old bars, cheese shops, trattorie (including Bruno e Sandro or is it Sandro e Bruno? – both have moustaches) leading right down to San Sebastiano with its painted twisting columns and organ doors by Veronese.

No, we are not to be deflected from our purpose, and fortified we stride over the bridge in the right-hand corner, down the fondamenta (not flooded this time – it often is), noting the striking art-deco brass name-plate of the artist Teodoro Wolf-Ferrari, and arrive at the very splendid land entrance gate to the Ca' Rezzonico. Luck is with us. It is actually open when it claims to be. (Such accuracy is far from being the case throughout Italy.) We enter the noble Baroque portal: immediately to the left is a grand niched fountain with the crowned Rezzonico arms carved in a curvy, asymmetrical shield. On axis with this, the androne – that is the large through-room directly behind the main entrance from the canal – has been closed for years. The shallow stairs are solemn, the walls Naples yellow, grey and plaster pink, but it is only on the landing that we get our first intimation of what is to come. Our introduction to grandeur, frivolity and Mannerism comes in the form of a little putto with the most petulant of expressions pouting at the turn of the stair. He is either pulling down or pulling off his little fur hat, and his expensive fur cape manages to reveal more than it covers. The little chap (his brother?) at the top of the stairs has the right idea. He is perched on a barrel and is gaily proffering a fluted cup of wine. He makes a fitting introduction to the first room which is the pink and grey ballroom. It astonishes.

Here almost everything is painted to deceive the eye. A smattering of real architecture is wittily introduced to keep you guessing. Light floods in, filtered through octagonal-paned windows and ruched curtains, and is further warmed by reflections from the pink building opposite. Your eye is distracted from the two

COMUNE DI VENEZIA
MUSEO CIVILE
CA' REZZONICO
MUSEO DEL SETTECENTO VENEZIANO
GUARDIA DI FINANZA

great gilt-wood chandeliers by the set of extraordinary furniture: although sparsely placed, as befits a ballroom, each piece is so opulent and complex that the mind boggles. Nine guéridons of naked negroes with very white eyes have intricately carved chains of boxwood around their necks. The arms and legs of the chairs are fashioned as writhing tree trunks with tiny piccaninnies lying swaddled in the branches, and the Moorish slaves supporting them wear feather skirts. There is a tripod of yapping gryphons. The whole suite is completely mad. The next room begins the enfilade towards the Grand Canal. Brocade flounces and curtains have recently been restored to the succession of doors and very pretty they look.

The ceiling is a ravishing Tiepolo, celebrating a grand Rezzonico marriage. How well he painted the shot fabrics, and what love of striped material. There are a hundred details that enchant. He did it after his return from Würzburg where he created the most beautiful staircase I have ever seen. The pretty little oratory all grey and white swirls that is built out from this room contains an odd piece of rococo hinged furniture that somehow converts its use from sitting to praying. It does not in the least resemble a shooting stick. A succession of other rooms leads into the oddly disappointing portego – the central room on the piano nobile. The balcony windows are open so we can step out into the dazzling light and be enchanted by the rooftops, the brilliance, the busy activity on the Grand Canal. The Palazzo Grassi nearly opposite looks very plain and dull, newly cleaned and restored with its blind plate-glass windows. Curiously, it was by the same architect, Masari, who completed the Ca' Rezzonico after Longhena's death.

Back inside, another sort of brilliance can be savoured by standing underneath the huge Murano-glass chandelier in the room next to the ballroom. Here you see an intricate coloured world of vitrified fountains, opalescent white and grey turning higher into concentric sprays of particoloured flowers, bright blue and pink carnations and yet more feathery red, yellow and green ones dangling.

Up the oddly steep, unadorned staircase, we reach the second piano nobile where there is so much to enjoy it is difficult to know where to begin. We make straight for Carrie's favourite room, the Sala dei Longhi. This airy and gracious room has windows on two sides, is hung with bright yellow silk bordered in lacquer red, and contains thirty paintings by Longhi. We are transported back to the charming artificial eighteenth-century Venetian world of carnival cloak and mask. Painted in crumbly pastel colours, doll-like ladies in panniers hold levees, receiving procurators, priests, portrait-painters, dressmakers, singing and dancing tutors. In slightly stiff poses they don tricorns and black lace cloaks and, accompanied by cicisbeos in domino masks, they visit convents, rhinoceroses and the Ridotto. A strange chalky vermilion and green predominates, punctuated by the black of the wraps and almost abstract triangular hats. They evoke the sound of the mandolin, but there is also something sinister in those bone-white masks projecting from the blackness like the upper skull of a baboon, and in the frightening simple oval of pitch-black in the middle of a pale doll-like face. They serve to remind us of the darker side of our natures and that the tinkling sound of carnival cloaks melancholy, tragedy and despair.

When I first knew these paintings they were hung in the eighteenth-century manner from the cornice on long yellow and red ribbons, with outbursts of rosettes. They are now suspended on ugly metal rods attached to a brutal metal box object cutting into the cornice. Why? If it is some sort of security device it is intrusive and ham-fisted in the extreme. Also the pictures are now lit by an unsubtle modern system jutting out like ugly angle-poises. This has happened recently to almost all the museums in Venice, and is very sad. It is in line with the crass and insensitive approach of museums throughout Europe, inflicting on the collections their conception of Modernity. It is this mentality that ruthlessly scrubs paintings till they glow like colour-slides, whilst painting any given polychrome decorations a uniform tasteful grey.

At the end of this enfilade is a lovely alcoved bedroom hung with faded brown wallpaper dottily repeating the Arch of Titus in Rome, and beyond this in the corner a memorable little antechamber painted with a solitary falcon swooping on a fleeing flock of sparrows. It is our introduction to the haunting world of Gian Domenico Tiepolo. But first it leads us into a tiny stuccoed reconstructed 'cabinet', cloudy-glinting with old looking-glass and carved with grapes and flowers painted mulberry, ochre and green against a warm white background.

When we have recovered, we retrace our steps and, crossing to the other side, enter the even more magical series of small rooms decorated by Domenico Tiepolo. They were transplanted here from Tiepolo's own villa on the mainland, the Villa Zianigo. The series is dominated by 'Il Mondo Nuovo' – the New World – which, though modest in size, must be one of the oddest and most poignant of frescoes. A group of rather lumpen spectators is watching some mysterious event, the ladies with uneven hems: they have their backs to you so you become one of the spectators yourself and almost start straining over their shoulders to see what is happening. It is like one of those moments in a Fellini film when the entire cast lines up on a beach and stares inexplicably out to sea. Like Fellini, there is a smattering of clowns and hints of circus tents. A man is doing something with a pole, and one of the crowd half-turns to you, enigmatically. It is painted in thin, nervous strokes and has a pastel patina.

In the other rooms are capriccios, burlesques and caricatures, all enlivened with a nervy outline. Absurd ladies in overblown bonnets walk whippet dogs. In the Camera dei Pagliacci we look up at masked craggy buffoons clad in loose white clothes and wearing attenuated white conical hats which combine to produce jumpy, abstract jauntiness. They perform acrobatics on tightropes and swings, and stay in the mind forever.

An utterly different, but still completely Venetian, mood is struck round the corner by the two Canalettos newly hung in the Portego dei Dipinti. There are barely any others in Venice – the National Gallery in London has the best collection – but this pair can be studied with the greatest of pleasure. The view from the Ca' Foscari right up the Grand Canal to the Rialto has been stupidly cropped in the Palazzo's guide-book to make nonsense of its bold composition. Like most paintings by Canaletto the mood is dominated by an intense luminous strong sky. According to my friend Edmund, the artist obtained this effect with the almost exclusive use of black, but J. G. Links more convincingly points out that Canaletto bought a particularly expensive sort of Prussian blue. What cannot be disputed is the dashed-on broad streak of red in the sky – it is masterly. And the painting of the buildings: first a base coat of rawish umber, quite loosely put in, then an intensely realistic, almost photographic network of detail lovingly inscribed in various darker shades of brown or, as Edmund would say, black. For these I think he must have used a ruler. I am also convinced that he used some sort of camera or optical device to gain these effects: Links disputes this by saying each picture is not physically accurate since it is often made up from three or more viewpoints. But that is precisely what a camera does – even from the same spot you can move it round and get separate views which can then be combined into a larger composition. Also, I feel the way Canaletto composes paintings, with their abrupt and unusual terminations, derives from a framed optical device. It is how you would see things if you looked through an empty frame. None of this really matters because the finished paintings are so good, and even with such a wealth of intricacy and incident the detail does not predominate and the paintings remain essentially painterly.

It is time to leave the Ca' Rezzonico. I have never ever known the third floor open, so regard the marionette theatre, costumes and pharmacy shops lovingly described in detail by the Sitwells as an elaborate myth. In a way it may be a relief as we find ourselves outdoors again on the fondamenta, our minds reeling with thoughts of masks, dominoes, gaming rooms, spinets, slaves, brocades, Tiepolos and Canaletto's use of black. We never thought for a moment of Browning.

We cross back briefly into the little campo on our way to the Campo Santa Margherita, in order to admire and possibly even buy something from the market boats moored on the Rio di San Barnaba. The brightly-coloured barges are filled with neat boxes of white asparagus, blood oranges, strawberries, artichokes complete with their huge floppy thistle-leaves, pears, onions, lemons, huge white mushrooms, fennel, aubergines, spinach, cauliflowers and pots of basil. Large brown awnings are slung above to give shade from the sun, and the whole effect is extraordinarily picturesque. The boats are called *Walter*, *Terri*, *Mario I* and *Mario II*, all in those traditional nautical stencilled letters, and colouring that is still the same as on the barges on the Seine in Paris, as on boats in Brittany, in Cornwall, and on the wherries at New Malden in Essex.

A man struggles with a very large trolley of vegetables over the steps of the bridge. At the top he has to turn round, and bump the burden down backwards. He reminds me of the time when I had to do much the same with a small, but heavy, child in a push-chair. Just on the left is a shop where you can buy masks of Verdi and Wagner. In the Campo we head straight for my favourite local café, wending obliquely through market stalls, newspaper stands and a ramshackle little hut in the centre filled with space-invader machines and lire-in-the-slot bucking broncos. The small café has a large red sign outside with swaggering art-nouveau lettering. Inside, the simple white walls have mirrors with white stylized roses like Rennie Mackintosh mouldings. It has a marble counter and is dominated at the other end by a great gleaming copper and bronze coffee urn, the finest in the city.

Under the crested bronze eagle on top, the polished dome reflects the coloured glass ceiling, and the copper pink sides multiply the rows of multicoloured bottles behind the bar. Within the dome cups are kept warm and there are various pipes and nozzles protruding from the main body to foam milk and other coffee frothings. It gurgles and hisses and slightly steams like an old engine as the driver expertly works the valves to provide my espresso and Carrie's cappuccino. As we are leaving, an old friar shuffles in, wrapped in a long brown scarf, clutching a large sack. He is wearing tartan carpet slippers.

A few doors down is a wonderfully loony shop, crammed with treats for the ephemerist. Edmund, who knows my tastes, would snort and walk quickly by but I love to linger and savour the oddest mixture in the window of deco pencil boxes, Swiss chalets, old bottles of perfumed ink, and bronzed roundels of 3-D Madonnas. Today there has been added a superb series of scenes from *The Yellow Submarine* neatly hand-copied onto shaped plywood. Inside, the locals buy lottery tickets and cigarettes surrounded by piles of old postcards, greetings cards and notebooks like the ones in which this account is being written. This particular one says 'Quaderno' copybook on the cover and must date from about 1933. As if scenes from *The Yellow Submarine* were not treat enough, today the shop is even more cramped than usual with a quite extraordinarily large object placed in the middle. You have to squeeze past it to get at the postcards, knocking over as you do a pile of religious diaries. It is shaped like a juke box with chrome decoration. It contains a bright green plastic hen with bri-nylon day-glo pink punk hair. When a coin is placed in the slot, the hen revolves for a bit, clucking, and out of an orifice in the machine pops a little plastic egg. In it, a faded slip of paper tells your fortune. There is an old man serving behind the counter; his youthful assistant has a shoulder-length cascade of bright shiny black curls cut in exactly the right Renaissance manner. He comes straight out of the Carpaccios we are shortly to see and, what's more, he knows that we know. Local youths circle outside on bicycles.

In our youth, we used to scour the square in search of the best value Menu Turistico, and would eat our *misto di mare* and drink our thin *litro di bianco* sitting outside at night. We first met a friend in a café there. These days he is almost a judge but then he was dressed from head to foot as a jester. And it was not even carnival time.

The Scuola Grande Santa Maria del Carmelo tucked away just around the corner has a heavily-encrusted stuccoed steep pair of stairs leading to a magnificent room, the ceiling painted by Tiepolo in his most warm airy manner. It contains the famous incident of the scaffolder falling into the willing arms of a passing angel. It is such a pleasure to gaze down into the mirrors provided which reflect the creamy scenes above. These alternate with pink, pistachio and ochre stucco panels. There is nothing more bathetic

than to enter the next chamber with its deeply-carved rather primitive ceiling surrounded by gruesome paintings of the Martyrdom of the Maccabees. One brother is hideously recoiling on being shown the twin pincers that are about to gorge out his eyes, surrounded by a foreground of decapitations, severed hands, etcetera. Another painting has the evocative title 'Abigail assuages David who is enraged with her husband Nabal'. Novels could be written on such a theme – it would not be difficult for them to be better than the paintings.

The church next door, the Carmini, is still in restoration. A black mosquito net suspended low above the nave causes everything to be seen through a murky gauze as in an old-fashioned pantomine. The piers of the nave encased in blue-painted scaffolding further blur, making the whole interior seem a constructionist's maze, both misty and spidery, a cage and a net.

Down the Rio dei Carmini is the enormous Palazzo Zenobio, now in the hands of the Armenian order, whose interior I long to see. From photographs it looks almost better than the Rezzonico. The twin towers of San Angelo Raffaele announce a great formless barn of a building, shabby and falling down. Like many churches, inside it is disfigured by myriad strident tango-orange posters (*un pane per amore di Dio*), amplification and microphones, and enormous plastic pots of aspidistras clustered at random. A statue of the Virgin with an electric fairy-light halo is recessed in a grotto surrounded by flaming hearts.

Recoiling, I walk back through a campo with longish grass growing out of the cracks in the paving and cross a bridge. By chance I look back and see a perfect composition. Ordinary but as redolent I hope as Canaletto's straightforward views out of his studio window, reproduced in Link's book. I cannot explain how but something slots into place. One Christmas a whole group of us daily tried vaguely to visit San Sebastiano. Circumstances intervened. Early starts were difficult. Besides grappa hangovers there was caffè corretto in the café nearby and the church rigidly closed at noon. We never made it, and had to console ourselves in the local trattoria, warm and welcoming, serving all sorts of things not seen by the tourist in summer. A barge passes filled with the complete contents of a house, tables upturned, with a mattress on top on which sits the owner. Today in spring we find San Sebastiano astonishingly open. Directly inside the door the sign says in English, 'Sacred Place. Be Silent. No Shorts and No Low-Necked Dresses PLEASE!' Inside, a nun is polishing the plastic protection of the altar-cloth. The sacristan in a shabby coat thrusts a crumpled cyclo-styled sheet-guide in German, but nothing can distract from the noble coffered ceiling and organ case. Painted barley-sugar columns appear above the lattice grilles of the surrounding choir and mingle with the statues around the balcony. The great glory is the organ case, doors open, revealing an arch with festoons of horns and violins twined with golden ribbon and held aloft by red-ochre cherubs. On the inside of the open doors Veronese confines his figures to the lower third of both compositions, filling the rest with stately architecture. This has the effect of concentrating and heightening the drama. He has a particular ravishing use of blue, and vibrant warm greys and a pink that is almost a pale crimson.

The chapel to the left of the altar has a majolica floor in bright blue and orange, with tiles of pigs, birds, rabbits, spectacles and flagons of wine. They add an unexpected note of gaiety but, glancing up from the tomb of Veronese into a dark corner under the organ loft, a chubby but resolute cherub determinedly grasps a skull to his bosom.

It is such a short distance down the canal to the boat stop that I yield to temptation. Taking a number eight, we are very soon on the Riva degli Schiavoni. In summer this wide promenade is unbearably choked with trippers wearing Benetton clothes. Today it is almost empty, and the high water slaps happily over the white stone kerb of the riva bathed in gentle spring light. The bobbing gondolas still wear their bright plaid winter woollies over the seats. I love the litany of fine fubsy tugs moored here and repeat their names: *Novus*, *Strenuus*, *Sirius*, *Hippos* and *Squalus*. By chance I notice a plaque set into a wall of the Londra Palace Hotel commemorating the fact that Tchaikovsky composed his fourth symphony here in 1877. It is extraordinary how an artist always carries his country in his head and that such archetypal dark Russian sounds were created here amongst the shimmer and bustle.

The rustication just above water-level of the back of the Doges' Palace is set in diamonds like those on the fragment of the unfinished Ca' del Duca on the Grand Canal. Every other diamond is reversed so you get a pattern of diamonds sticking out, which curiously echoes in geometry and stone the glinting ripple of water below. This pleasing rhythm of rustication is only broken by the odd stone having fallen out and its dark cavity forming a perfect hole for pigeons, so every so often you see a little anxious beak sticking out of the blackness.

We pass the Indian red gothic Palazzo Dandolo, now the Danieli Hotel. Shades of Ruskin and Proust step in, and more recently that of Britten who wrote his last and strangest opera there: if we follow them we find ourselves in the most extraordinary foyer, like some lush reconstruction of a Venetian Palace for an early Hollywood movie. It makes me shudder and run out. There is such pleasure turning the corner from the Doges' Palace into the Piazzetta with the astonishing polychrome jumble of the south front of San Marco, the clock tower piled behind and the three flagpoles unfurling their pennants just as in a painting by Sickert. Quickly crossing the square we enter the courtyard of the Museo Archeologico under the Sansovino Library. You can always get away from people here – it is usually completely empty which is part of its charm. The courtyard has large Mannerist doric pilasters and is dominated by a huge white statue under a colonnade. It has faded yellow-ochre walls and you could well be in Rome. The noise from the Piazza reverberates around the arcades and filters into the museum like the sounds from a far-off swimming pool. Inside there is a feeling of remote stillness and calm. The cream walls are a foil for cream statues that are filled with passion – the passion of love, self-love, drunkenness and death.

There are statues of Eros, Narcissus, Dionysos and Satyr. Under a marbled frieze and elaborate ceiling painted with flowers lie dying gladiators. Whilst I look at the entangled 'Leda and the Swan', café music starts up in the Piazza below on the dot of eleven. It is as if their strange love-making were accompanied by the sounds of piano-accordions. The carvings have an extraordinary range of facial expression: jolly ladies, pensive boys, terrified warriors at the point of death. They are also strong in the feeling of movement: a fragment captures the twist of a rather stout lady's torso. Another room is entirely filled with busts on two tiers around the walls. Their heavy, sensual faces are those of Emperors, and Emperors' wives, one with a shiny black draped headdress. Frivolously, we try to recognize friends or film stars in their faces, a game slightly complicated by several having lost their noses.

Quadri's band begins to play 'Hello, Dolly' – perhaps that is what the swan was saying to Leda.

Back on the ground, we perversely turn right in order to obtain my favourite introduction to San Marco, and walk the noble shabby arcade, patinated columns on one side matching pilasters on the other, bronze lanterns above, cloudy glass globe lamps to the side, and cherry and white marble laid in diamond pattern underfoot. Café life is in full swing. The café soon passed on our right has a suave cocktail pianist and we can just hear traces of the bands in the Piazza. Is there anywhere else in the world that still provides so much live music in such a concentration of place? Its many moods and abrupt changes, wistful to jolly, haunting to waltzing, always reminds me of the film music of Nino Rota.

We turn the corner and step out to admire the façade of the Zecca, or mint, also by Sansovino. Next to it, there used to be a huge granary, which was swept away in Napoleon's improvements. It was his only mistake. Although the gardens and trees replacing it are agreeable enough and the iron-work surrounding them magnificent and neo-classical in the extreme, the backs of buildings unintended for view lie exposed. What cities need are buildings, and this simple brick building, with its prickly lattice-work crenellations and strange, attenuated gothic central arch, provided a foil to its grander brother, the Doges' Palace, on the other side of the Piazzetta. It can be seen to best advantage in Canaletto's paintings (reproduced in Links' book) of the Molo looking both east and west. If I ruled it would be rebuilt. Its loss, however, is compensated for by the exquisite Napoleonic casino at the end of this promenade. It was designed by Lorenzo Santi and is the most rarefied building in Venice. At the moment the lettering AIR TERMINAL is falling off, and it is derelict.

Harry's Bar is a received opinion, so we turn right by it and, passing the old Ridotto, and shirt and chandelier shops, turn right again at the top, firmly resisting the temptation to enter the square immediately by the Bocca di Piazza, but following the Napoleonic wing (from the back it looks like Naples) to the left, until we can turn and walk through the entrance in the centre of this wing. The grandest staircase sweeps off on one hand, and San Marco, slightly at an angle in the distance, is framed by a dignified forest of columns and arches. At our feet is inlaid the outline of the façade of

Sansovino's San Germiniano. It was ill-fatedly positioned in several places within the evolving Piazza – the obsessive can map its progress from inlaid inscriptions in the square – until it came to rest before oblivion as an awkward buffer between the Procuratie Vecchie and the disparate Procuratie Nuove.

Ascending the monumental staircase we are overwhelmed by Santi's rich neo-classical decoration, honey-coloured and grey. This was the State Entrance to the Royal Palace of Napoleon leading directly to the immense white and gold ballroom set about with chandeliers. It could almost be the Winter Palace in St. Petersburg. Unfortunately it is now used for exhibitions of modern art and is inevitably partitioned by stark white screens and low false ceilings. The entrance galleries and the following two rooms constitute the finest series of Empire rooms, decorated in the Pompeian style. Delicate fans are painted in the gentle cove of the ceiling. The dado is painted a chalky green and mauve to imitate marble, and my favourite view of the Piazza below is through the draped muslin curtains at the windows. At the end of the Galleria a little corridor has been closed off from view, and used as a storeroom. Peeping behind the curtain you discover the most exquisite Etruscan decorations painted in orange ochre like Hamilton vases.

In the first room the Empire decoration is perfectly in keeping with the sculpture of Canova, but the original scagliola and marble plinths have recently been replaced by cubist creations in teak and perspex. It is only repeating what has been done at the British Museum. Inside an ugly plastic box is the small plaster version of Canova's pyramid monument to Titian. It is the first of all three that we will visit.

The next room has an almost cobwebby patina with its slate-grey marbled dado, cloudy mirrors and gilding. The fine lines of clear viridian green placed next to the gold define and enliven the ceiling. Pompeian dancers are painted on panels, their ribbons frozen around them like art-nouveau hula-hoops. In the centre of the room a tripod table of bronze sphinxes with mono-paws holds up a Wedgwood-blue table made of cameos. It is guarded by a festoon of green rope supported on sticks which unintentionally gives it a festive, spindly air.

Elated but exhausted we decide to leave the rest of the collection

for another time, and make our way back through the arcades and round to Florian's.

We push open the familiar loved double-doors with their elegant S-shaped polished brass handles. Disused, dented, tarnished cylindrical coffee percolators stand on either hand. An evocative series of miniature painted rooms fans out on both sides, crimson and gold, and the enfilade is repeated to infinity by the cloudy mirrors in dark elaborate frames placed at either end. Each casket-room, faded and worn, has a different theme, Turkish, Gothic, evoked by panels of tempera paintings with filigree borders all behind glass, reflecting the glitter of bunches of frilly wall lights.

Even the ceilings are covered in glass, smoke-darkened, enmeshed in geometrical borders of complicated Turkish patterns. Designed by Ludovico Cadorin in 1858, it typifies that mid-nineteenth-century mood which we hear in the music of Verdi. But it is not Verdi we actually hear. The band outside has just begun to play 'Perfidia'. We sink down on the ox-blood banquettes and order hot chocolate from a waiter in a wing collar. The elegant silver tray is placed on the marble table, as the trio wittily plays 'Tea for Two' in an amusingly detailed, complicated arrangement involving extensive use of pizzicato. They are having fun, and we are sharing it. 'Blue Moon' is given a more conventional treatment with the rather thin violin soaring in the manner of Stéphane Grappelli. The violinist has a permanent smile on his face, the instrument tucked neatly into the folds of his neck. During the next torrid Hungarian number his eyebrows shoot up as if in amazement at his own virtuosity. Frenzies of slithering glissandi calm to a lilting Magyar melody: in turn this melancholy is soon shattered by a burst of frantic abandon, when the rasping cello saws and pants. Such schizophrenic Zigeunerei can be a little unnerving when trying to sip your chocolate. As if satiated by this storm in your cocoa, a high tremolo brings the music to a rousing end. The musicians get up and bow to the patter of applause. Politely on cue, the band from Quadri's across the square now start playing swing on clarinets.

The beauty of these cosy little painted chambers at Florian's is that the fourth side is open to the Piazza so that, whilst still being enclosed, you can look out to all the toing and froing. Today, the waiters' gold epaulettes on their white jackets flash in the sun.

How different is the scene in winter when the square is emptier but never quite deserted. I have been there at one o'clock in the morning and seen a lone reveller crossing in a cloak. I have been there at dawn and seen a solitary sweeper. The only time I have seen it completely empty of people was during *acqua alta* when it was filled with quite choppy waves. We had to walk slowly in single file over duckboards to the Piazzettas.

Less drastic but still dramatic flooding takes place in the winter and I can recall my excitement on first seeing little lakes collected in the irregular surface of the pavement. You could stand on the edge and look down on the clear, gently rippling surface to see upside-down arcades and beyond their reflection to the white lines of Istrian stone let into the grey paving. It was like a mirage of some fabulous oriental palace and I was transfixed. When I was drawing it, a French schoolgirl came up and looked over my shoulder, nosily. 'It's just like a photograph,' she said dismissively to her companions as they walked away.

Once, in winter, I was walking down the arcade and chanced on the most peculiar sight in Florian's. In the larger furthest room a café concert was taking place, and just as I was about to pass they began to play one of my favourite songs, Erik Satie's 'Tendrement'. I stopped and stared through the glass which filtered the sound as if through water. The singer was very young and thin and dressed as a 'twenties vamp in black sequins and a feather. She had huge black staring eyes and neither they nor the rest of her moved as her mouth motioned like a fish. Through a screen of orange gladioli I peered at the audience of wrinkled old ladies clamped in their furs, leopard, cheetah and ocelot. Grotesquely made-up, cowering under a mauve wig, one old lady held a long rope of pearls motionless. What was so eerie was that only the pianist's arms and singer's mouth moved – the rest were as waxwork. Very strange and more Philippe Jullian than Proust.

We continue down the arcade and turn at the top to admire Sansovino's Loggetta. It is spring again and stalls sprout, selling gondoliers' hats gay with ribbon, headscarves, and lurid plastic gondolas which light up, complete with 3-D Rialto backdrop. Examining the exquisite Loggetta it is difficult to believe that it is a piecing together of fragments after the original was crushed when the Campanile fell down in 1902.

In the early 1970s this was chosen to be the first building to be cleaned by the British Venice in Peril Fund, using all the latest fancy techniques. It emerged polychrome with pink Verona marble surrounding white reliefs and the variegated marble projecting columns offsetting patinated green bronze statuary in niches. Unfortunately, to protect this new richness the stone was injected with some sort of silicone which has left it with the dull patina of plasticine. It strikes me that once a building or a picture has been cleaned even now modern science has not found a way of protecting the delicate new surface satisfactorily. Conservation is still in the dark ages and is extremely controversial. Whilst no one can deny the success of the restored entrance to the Doges' Palace – the Porta della Carta – just opposite the Loggetta, I was horrified recently to go through it and see the newly-cleaned Giants' Staircase. The beautiful bone-white Istrian stone is one of the major beauties of Venice. Whether fashioned into statues, palaces, kerbs, or simple lintels around humble windows this pure whiteness both sets off and keys the colours all around. Also it weathers to a pleasing sooty blackness in places, which further sets its whiteness into relief. The staircase has been restored to a warm sort of beige which ruins the whole monochrome of the courtyard. If the pristine whiteness cannot be preserved intact the restorers should wait until science proves certainly that it can. It is dubious injecting silicone into a human old body, but into a building, which lasts longer, it is a crime.

As more and more of the restored façade of San Marco re-emerges from its long sojourn behind boards, some of the colours are quite startling, the greens and porphyry-reds of the columns on the central porch for instance. But how long will they retain their colour? I love the way some make no pretence of supporting anything and are simply there to add to the opulence, just as the spindly arches at either end, supported on one column and then on a cluster, have no function other than to lengthen the façade. The new gilding is entirely successful. I remember seeing the golden haloes of the apostles and saints with pin-pricks of light shining through them, like a colander. This effect only happens for a moment at dawn.

How disappointing the nineteenth-century mosaics are, really hardly better than the religious postcards from the kitsch-shop in

the Campo Santa Margherita. What a nightmare for Ruskin to have lived to see what he had most loved destroyed in the restorations of the 1870s! The north façade still retains that lifeless mechanical look that characterizes the Victorian restoration of buildings throughout Europe. Only the carved roundels retain the spiritual beauty of hand-craftsmanship. Unfortunately, our own age has done no better. The scandalous replacement of the bronze horses has left us with reproductions with all the surface beauty of fibre-glass. As Peter Lauritzen convincingly argues in his excellent book *Venice Restored*, there was no valid reason for their removal in the first place. These proud creatures had survived remarkably well exposed to fresh air for at least 1,600 years, only to be crammed into a humiliatingly meagre enclosed space subject to the pollution of close proximity to a constant stream of visitors. These burnished golden horses have stood for 700 years as a symbol of the mighty Venetian empire: it is tragic that the restored thriving Venice should be typified by lifeless replicas.

I enter the basilica by the Porta dei Frari under the hanging blankets in the transept. All is rich and mystical. Had I entered earlier the whole church would have reverberated with the sound of a hundred vacuum-cleaners. However efficient, they never remove the overwhelming smell of damp dog which seems embedded in the fabric. Could it simply be the smell of stale incense, or the residue of all the pork fat that an art historian told me was assiduously rubbed into the marble walls for centuries to add lustre?

Every time Sickert painted Venice indoors I feel it must have been raining and, although I have always loved his rich umbrageous interiors of San Marco, it was a shock when I first saw the real thing to realize his redolent browns and ochres were in fact sumptuous gold, which glows amber in the sunlight. Again and again you do not know where to look, there is so much to absorb, from the mosaics in the domes lit with tiny windows like stars, to the undulating fields of tessellation under-foot, so marvellously evoked by Proust. This beautiful landscape is further enriched by the strewing of Turkey carpets all over the nave, so the whole floor becomes a subtle shimmer, pattern upon pattern, of intricate fabric on intricate stone.

Lorenzetti is incomparable and I choose at random: 'The vast iconographical scheme of the mosaics of St. Mark corresponds to an immense, but harmonious and well-thought-out plan to which we cannot really attribute a name unless we are inclined to accept the ancient tradition which makes the author of it the Calabrian abbot Gioachino da Santa Fiora who is remembered by Dante as having been gifted with prophetic powers, and who, according to some chronicles, lived for many years in the basilica itself to be able to look after the vast work.' As, I immediately think, did Gaudi at the Sagrada Familia in Barcelona, whose curious bauble-pinnacles so oddly resemble the three-dimensional Greek crosses that top the domes here at San Marco. We are in the atrium, on our way out, looking up, lost in the frozen, moving Byzantine world in mosaic. Round the corner, workmen are lumbering a stepped primitive wooden device like that used for storming mediaeval cities, to attend to some minor upkeep of the fabric.

The little alleyways nearby are choked with souvenirs. We push through on our way to Santa Maria Formosa – past the tiny hotel I first stayed at when I was eighteen, with its unexpected view down the canal to the Bridge of Sighs. The shops begin to display huge cellophane-wrapped Easter eggs, whose bright top-knots flower into asses' rather than rabbits' ears. The biggest we find is two feet six inches tall and is covered with marzipan doves and nests, silk flowers and pink ribbons, and is standing on a silver ring. It costs an impressive L.160,000.

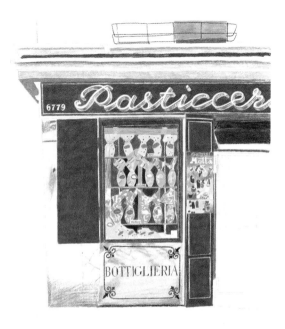

Sickert's painting of Santa Maria Formosa hung in our local art gallery and made such an impression on me as a child – showing a different world of sparkle and shadow – that I longed to visit the real place. It is one of Coducci's most impressive churches, lucid in its simplicity, and a little plaque tells that it was rebuilt after being shelled by the Austrians in 1916.

Today the church is humming with activity as the whole local neighbourhood prepares it for Easter celebration. Ladies are busy with vacuum-cleaners whilst the men lay down heavy floral carpets, great armfuls of flowers – gladioli and lilies – are arranged in homely vases. No sooner is a carpet laid out than a lady in slacks appears and busily starts hoovering it. There must be about fifty people in the church, not counting all the babies and children, eight hoovers and a score of brooms. A lady with bouffant grey hair is elaborately arranging the corners of the immaculately-laundered altar cloth. Everyone seems remarkably happy and, as we leave, a team starts erecting what looks like rather a large octagonal swimming pool in the baptistery.

Outside in the campo there are a few market stalls. On our honeymoon we used to buy figs here and eat them by the side of the canal. Occasionally gondoliers would pass and smile at us.

The Palazzo Querini-Stampalia contains the most quirky and charming collection in Venice. You enter from across the bridge and are surrounded by an inexplicable modernist fantasy. Although I admire Scarpa's work elsewhere I do not feel a fine Venetian Palace deserves this dotty treatment of stepping stones and marble troughs. You almost expect a bonsai island or at least a significant pebble in this atmosphere of Cubism meeting Zen. The gallery is on the third floor and if, like me, you hate lifts and slog up the steep stair you will find the large heavy door at the top invariably locked. When you finally get into the gallery, you enter one of the most enchanting rooms with chandeliers, light rococo panels painted pink and pistachio, the white dots in the shiny smooth terrazzo floor like fossilized hail. In front of the bottle-glass windows overlooking the canal sits an eighteenth-century sofa with wide almond-green stripes. From here you can see the gently bending enfilade which follows the curve of the canal. Like many of the more enjoyable places in Venice, you will find it empty, so will be free to wander in peace. Here there are topographical

views, Longhis, pastel-painted plasterwork with incised borders of garlands and flowers. There is a pink room with a magnificent set of neo-classical Klismos chairs decorated in Etruscan red, and the prettiest room is the closet beyond the bedroom in the wing at the back. You have to unhook the crimson cord to see this. At the moment it is undergoing restoration and I fear its delicate bloom will be lost.

The organ is playing Mozart as we enter San Zaccaria, filled with white and pink flowers for Easter. We look at the tinted eighteenth-century engravings of the Stations of the Cross, waiting for the party being shouted at by their guide around the Bellini to move on and preferably out. The church is a fusion of Gothic and Lombardic, a combination of the old world and the new. Raised upon rather awkwardly attenuated Mannerist bases, the columns have capitals made from carved eagles, their wings outstretched to support the volutes. The lower arches around the apse are Renaissance, reverting back to a pointed Gothic on the second tier.

We place our 200-lire coin in the slot and the Bellini suddenly glows orange, green and blue-ish pink out of the gloom. It makes the other paintings in the church look inept. You are immediately struck by the power of the composition, but also by its grace. All the faces, unlike the rest which is sharply painted, have a smudged, tender, spiritual quality. They all look away, immersed in their own remote worlds, except for the stern stone head of the keystone of the arch directly above the Virgin. He stares out menacingly and reminds us of all the hundreds of bold carved keystones throughout Venice whether fantastic or grotesque, noble or humorous. All the keystones of the Procuratie Nuove are different, for instance, but not noticed by Ruskin who was too busy examining the nearby capitals of the Doges' Palace. This carved flamboyance was never taken up in England, except in a very minor way in Queen Anne's Gate in London. Here an impish spirit is carved into the slightly primitive grotesque keystones, enlivening the neat trim brick fronts. As we leave San Zaccaria we pause to look in the crystal casket to the left of the door. In it, an effigy of the dead Christ lies on a ritzy brocade mattress surrounded by hundreds of tarnished filigree flaming hearts hanging from faded ribbon. In the midst of all this someone has devotedly hung a worn 1950s wristwatch.

We begin to curve round the familiar route on our way to the Scuola di San Giorgio degli Schiavoni. Thinking of keystones makes us notice other piquant details that are so typically Venetian: the black stencilled lettering painted on the white ground of the street signs, the houses numbered in white squares or ovals outlined in black, the numbers an Indian red. The ambiguous blobs of bright colour on walls seem applied at random as if a house-painter was trying out an essay in pointillism. These look even brighter after rain. The range of the fantasy we have observed in keystones is equally to be found in doorknobs. These usually go in pairs and can be ladies, lions, moors, blackamoors in turbans, gorgons, grimacing satyrs, or my favourite, which we just happen to be passing at No. 4717, a pair of sour-faced, thin-lipped nineteenth-century twin gentlemen with mutton-chop whiskers and high collars. The brother on the right is a little more highly polished through use.

Only a thin curtain separates the mundane calle from the glowing marvel just inside the Scuola di San Giorgio. The 'Sansovino' painted ceiling is a sort of vibrant gravy-colour with the flesh, green, rose and bluish-grey Carpaccios surrounding the chamber suffused in the warm amber light of the chunky uplighters. These actually resemble the leg holding up the table in St. Augustine's study, the first picture to draw our attention, its interior dark green with a crimson niche. Pen poised, sitting in his black cowl at his desk, the saint looks up out of the window, frozen forever in an attitude of revelation. The details are compelling: on his table a shell, a bell, a pair of scissors, an hour-glass under the table in an alcove, a manuscript book of music simply placed open at the bottom right-hand corner. Carpaccio signed his work on a trompe-l'oeil folded piece of paper, and in the next painting, the 'Death of St. Jerome', a little lizard on the step is sniffing this little note. It is these sorts of details that hold you rapt and enchanted. The 'St. Ursula' series in the Accademia, likewise, holds your attention with a wealth of anecdote and pictorial surprise, but somehow they lack warmth. This is partly due to the way they are hung, but chiefly a result of their hideous and cold restoration.

On our way to the Fortuny Museum we pause to look at patterned paper at the Legatoria Piazzesi. Here they use original printing blocks and water-based inks which slightly squidge round the edges when printed. It is difficult to know what to buy because I want everything. There are folders, and blotting pads, and hat-boxes, and portfolios all covered with these ravishing, often strange traditional patterns. There are also cartouches, book-plates and repeat-pattern papers in piles of festoons, phoenixes, gondolas, palaces and doves. We make our purchases (wrapped in even more repeat patterns) and leave. I realize I have expensive tastes.

Coming to the Campo San Stefano (or Morosini, as it is called) we really should turn right for the Fortuny, but we make a brief detour to the left to see the land-locked Palazzo Pisani. We approach down a little alleyway and through an arch which turns out to be a charming little flanking wing to the vast mass of the Palace. Children are playing football, thumping balls against its walls. We continue, dodging them, directly across the square under the arch on the other side, and enter a secret world.

Suddenly, from an upstairs window, a woman starts singing a phrase of Debussy, she repeats it again and again. Across the alley on the other side, a French horn begins to play an expressive melody. The Palazzo is now an academy of music and is always filled with these haunting and tantalizing fragments which make a surreal symphony. Further down the alley, and loveliest of all, a piano begins to play Fauré, whose music evokes the lapping and languor of Venice: this very piece may well have been written just across the canal in the Palazzo of the Princesse de Polignac. Thinking of her makes us recall Reynaldo Hahn's Venetian songs which he played sitting at a piano in her gondola at night. With Fauré still faintly in our ears, we pass the land entrance of the Palazzo Barbaro which in turn makes us think of Henry James and that wonderful dark rich interior Sargent painted of the Curtis family. Thinking of Sargent's dark interiors makes me think of his rapid, vivid watercolours. And thinking of all this makes me trip over a saucer of milk left for a cat. Through rusty grilles can be seen a very strange forgotten courtyard. It is stuffed with planks, headless statues, lavatory bowls and cats. Round the corner you enter a dark grotto filled with large statues and more cats, and from here another bend leads you to a tiny alley down to the Grand Canal itself. Turning back, you look through another arch up into the huge attenuated courtyard with perspectives of flying loggias, open arch upon open arch. It is one of the oddest architectural sights and is like a Piranesi, or more probably with its forlorn sinister undertones like a fantasy by James Pryde. Retracing our steps, slightly dazed, we hear the same phrase of Debussy still being repeated, and it is only the youths playing football that return us to the real world.

For some reason I have always found the Fortuny difficult to light upon – it would be easier by canal. Like everywhere else the museum is often, inexplicably, closed. As you walk up the external stair, covered in ivy and supports, you cannot help noticing how dilapidated it is, with bushes growing out of the cracks. On our first visit many years ago, Fortuny's old servant aged about ninety-three showed us around: the whole Palazzo had an air of Miss Haversham – beside cobwebs and rent fabrics there was thick dust and a feeling of decades of neglect. The elderly retainer would scuttle about, trying to light lamps unlit for years, and opening drawers filled with tiny pleated masses of faded splendour, like yarns of silk. 'Behold the dress of La Duse,' he would croak, playing up to his audience, undeterred by our limited comprehension. Thrilled, he demonstrated a model theatre whose cyclorama Fortuny had invented. 'Rheostats,' he said proudly in English as he demonstrated that electricity could simulate the gradual change from dawn to dusk. Dusk turned to night and, triumphantly flicking the final switch, he said, 'Ecco la luna!'

The next time I visited all had changed. White screens and spotlights were everywhere, blown-up photographs had didactic captions. I returned again to find it closed. Today, luckily, the original interior has reappeared but dusted and without the rents. The huge studio is divided by magnificent stencilled fabrics – recreations of the rich Renaissance fabrics of Veronese. They are a fusion of the mediaeval and oriental. Sometimes they even evoke the barbaric splendour of his native Spain. They are lit by Fortuny's own white areas of limelight and hanging lamps of his own design which are like a diminishing succession of inverted pagodas. What a wonderful man he was: painter, photographer, designer of fabric, stage sets and ladies' clothes, all with such fluidity and invention. There is a large painting by him of the studio. In it there is a suit of Japanese armour and a huge coloured cloth suspended from the ceiling; on the floor are oriental carpets, and light floods in from the main door. He himself is reflected in a mirror on the left. He has lovingly captured the rich glow of fabrics, old faded furniture, comfortable piles of cushions in the dappled light through bottle-glass windows.

If we follow the palace round through the campo and down the alley, we come out to a little landing and look up the Grand Canal at exactly the same viewpoint as that matchless painting by Richard Parks Bonington, except the real sky is not as good as the one he painted. Also, we can see how smartly the present Count Volpi keeps up his palace.

We cross the Rialto bridge, noticing how shabby the new cream colouring of the Fondaco degli Tedeschi – the post office – has already become. It always used to be a pleasing saturated Venetian pink. Stalls on either side sell trinkets and souvenirs, then wellingtons and tea-towels, and then come the vegetable stalls I love, so well described by Elizabeth David in her book on Italian cookery. Even when the stalls have gone, the area is imbued with an acetate vegetably smell. I walk through an arch and onto the banks of the Grand Canal. Opposite is the Ca' Civran now the home of the Guardia di Finanza. Back in the market little old ladies in polka-dot pinafores deftly chop the hearts out of artichokes. There is a stall entirely of courgette flowers with a proud notice, 'E arrivata la primavera dolcissime!!!!', followed by the more mundane, Kilo L.300.

A little further on is the fish market, housed under the arcade of a turn-of-the-century Gothic-revival building. It is in what I call the musical comedy style: Peter Lauritzen was very shocked when I told him that. He said, no, no, it was d'Annunzian. I was only thinking of *The Gondoliers*. There are other examples: the Palazzo Stern, the Casa Torres painted by my friend Dodd, and another artist's house near the youth-hostel on the Giudecca.

Fish fascinate. Here they lie glinting on beds of ice, eyes staring. Several stallholders have bare arms black to the elbow with ink of squid. I like these mounds of slimy blackness and particularly relish the curious rich taste somewhere between liquorice, Guinness and grouse.

Carrie goes off to shop and explore in a different direction and we arrange to meet for lunch. I take the traghetto across to the Ca' d'Oro. These giant gondolas, rowed by two, ferry the native Venetians across the Grand Canal. Everybody stands up in a line. You can always flatter yourself that you are a local, but do be warned there is nothing more humiliating than to fall over, and under no circumstances should a traghetto crossing be attempted with a hangover.

The marble of the Ca' d'Oro is all the colours of the inside of an oyster. It is indeed fairy-like and its Gothic is both airy and strong. This airiness provided Ruskin with one of his silliest explanations of the use of cable-moulding round the edges of the building. He said it looked like a parcel tied down with rope: had he ever tied up a parcel in his life he would have realised you wrap the string round the middle of the sides, not at the edges.

Water will be lapping into the lower arcaded loggia. The Ca' d'Oro has been undergoing restoration for years, and the finished result is completely disastrous. It has ruined the interior forever. Franchetti gave his collection to be seen in the context of a richly-decorated aristocratic home. Photographs show its original lay-out with brocades, carpets, tapestries, painted ceilings and stencilled walls creating a vibrant complexity. Needless to say, all this has been swept away and the rather indifferent collection isolated in a barren waste of modernity, spotlights and plate glass. Only the tiny oratory housing the Mantegna Saint Sebastian gives a hint of what it was like before, and even this has been given a silly modern lattice screen.

I begin walking up the Strada Nuova, a wide shopping street that I only really got to know when sharing an apartment in the Cannaregio region in winter with Edmund and Archibald. We used to meet and walk back together. Edmund paced on ahead, decisively, clutching his canvas and paints, looking neither to left nor right and resembling from behind the middle-period Beethoven with his great mane of hair. At home, in England, this mane usually has traces of gold leaf in it from picture-framing, and mud from the creation of his water-garden. Here however he had just dried his hands on it, having eaten a bowl of mussels. Following behind, Archie and I poked our grey heads into almost every shop, Archie looking for silk stockings, I for sweet labels. How different also was our approach to art. Archie stayed at home illustrating a Daphnis and Chloë peepshow whilst Edmund paced off to the same subject day after day, ruminated, then added a few strokes of the gentle sensitive colours beloved by the English Academy. I, on the other hand, wandering vague and dilatory, suddenly see a subject like the flash of a photograph and work swiftly to capture that vision on paper.

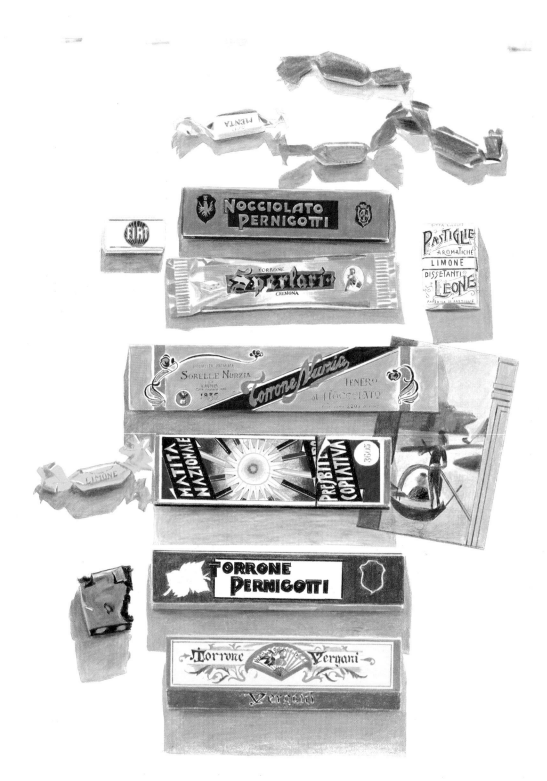

Now, as I cross the last bridge on the way to the Madonna dell' Orto, the great pediment of the Gesuiti looms up in the distance on the right, the details of its huge angels (supported by hundreds of iron brackets, which you can see from the Fondamenta Nuove) merging from afar into the spume of great waves, not unlike the stone froth around the top arches of San Marco, only larger.

The palace on the wide Fondamenta in the foreground has two tall, attenuated obelisks, one capped with a stone globe, the other missing globe replaced by a perched gull constantly there, serious and immobile, consciously trying to be a stone globe.

Inside the Madonna dell' Orto a cool, calm pink-grey light prevails. The famous Cima da Conegliano of St. John the Baptist just on the right is beautifully offset by the eighteenth-century Venetian Gothic confessional next to it. In it one could imagine Horace Walpole confessing all. Edmund once decided to paint quite a large picture of the interior and started to hack away at his roll of canvas. On the first day, however, he was sighted holding out an enormous board with this canvas tacked onto it, vainly trying to dab on the paint. This home-made board with its cruel nuts and bolts made the fingers bleed. He would not take his easel in with him because he said it did not show enough respect. Reason prevailed on the second day, but peace was shattered, alas, within moments by the great collapse of the easel on the slippery floor, combined with muffled yelps over spilt paint on marble.

A few days later he was still painting away during a funeral service when a muttering simpleton shuffled in, spied Edmund's palette and stuck his finger into a large dollop of Mars Violet, stared at it for a moment in wonder, and was just about to smear it over himself, the coffin and the entire church. Edmund, seeing this, simply shook his finger, firmly said 'Non!' and, taking a rag, calmly proceeded to clean the simpleton's finger.

Funeral boats are invariably moored opposite the campo in front of the Madonna dell' Orto. These distinctive black boats are encircled by a swagged festoon of bright yellow, and when in use two golden lions are placed in the bow. You see the boats filled with flowers making the all too short trip across to the cemetery island of San Michele. It is a journey we will be making later.

Mist blurs and blunts, the constant murmur of shoppers in the Strada Nuova muffled, and the usual rifle-fire of 'ciaos!' subdued to soft rockets rising slowly into the gentle haze. I walk on, loving this layer of blue-grey. The elaborate ironwork of the bridge to the Ghetto has simplified to a silhouette and the canal beyond merges into a mysterious nothingness. I pause on the bridge and out of this mysterious nothingness emerges a muffled-chugging barge laden with acqua minerale – water on water – soon followed by another boat bearing nothing but a solitary old gas stove. The sea-gulls mournfully cry, the tops of buildings are invisible. Ladies in furs and hats walk up and down the Fondamenta dei Ormesini; I cross the bridge and follow them. The first grocery shop on the right has a black and white tightly chequered floor, a more than half-closed venetian blind reluctantly lifted to show colourful tins of tonno, gamberetti, polpa di granchio, olio di oliva extra vergine, and finally Liberty Gold tins of peas to end up, heaven forbid, in risi e bisi. Next the cheese shop with displays of enormous octagonal boxes of Asiago placed on their end and on top of these carrier bags of Parmigiano containing a bright photograph of a crusty peek of cheese posing as Mont Blanc. These are joined by a swag of faded green paper chain left over from a Christmas many years ago.

Inside, the smiling cheeseman is happy to serve you ettos of innumerable different cheeses, and runs to a safe right at the back of the shop where he keeps our favourite Marscarpone.

Next door, the Fotocopie Riduzioni has an old-fashioned platen printing press, a few straggly geraniums, and is filled with examples of splendidly Victorian-looking 'Buon Natale' cards, cards for various trattorie and, most modern and forward-looking, a bold card for 'Claudia e Sandro Body Studio'.

A nun passes briskly.

Today a flower barge has moored by the Fondamenta. It is filled with those vile pot plants whose name I do not want to know and whose horrid green leaves turn at the top into an even worse red. I have a sudden mad desire to scuttle the boat and watch the slow sogging red sink into the putrid green waters.

The next, wonderfully decrepit shop is a faded bar, a deco espresso machine the only glimmer in the gloom. It has a window open onto the Fondamenta where groups of workers in blue overalls are handed out tall foaming glasses of Prosecco. A serrated poker-work sign says in primitive, hand-drawn capitals OGGI FRITELLE. But here every day is frying day.

Outside the Colore Ferramenta (nice old lettering, crimson on bottle green) hang yellow oilskins, blue plastic buckets, orange plastic brushes and green plastic flower pots. In the window they are trying out a minor essay in Christmas decoration, a twist of tinsel amongst the electric drills. The butcher next door has bought one of those pot-plant horrors and placed it in front of a neatly-hanging row of chickens, their scaly bright yellow claws frozen in cruel gesture, and hooked to an aluminium bar. Above the shop, a shutter creaks open and a lady begins her seasonal task of wrapping her window box in its winter plastic bag.

The little grocery has two festoons of garlic slung across the open window, pearly white against the dark inside. On the stall outside are banks of persimmons, Naples yellow apples, pink apples, clementines wrapped in garish paper, tiny cauliflowers and grapes. The old grocer (anorak and trilby) stands expertly trimming the bases of fennel bulbs with a sharpened table knife.

The following shop is so odd I do not know what it is. Peering through the grimy window I can just make out a surreal display of dusty plastic ballcocks, an electric fire (c.1953), a zinc chimney for a geyser and several lavatory-rolls metamorphosed by age into strange sagging baroque shapes.

Next is the popular bar constantly busy with the come and go of locals. Here they drink brandy, espresso and eat the occasional salty artichoke sandwich.

Another, slower nun passes the cover girls loudly displayed in the newsagent's next-door, black bows in their hair whilst swimming or rather posing in the sea. Besides *Il Giorno, Stampa Sera, Il Gazzettino*, sports papers and T.V. Mags, there are also displayed cigarette boxes, Tarot cards, transforming robots, 'lovely pet glow in the dark' toys for children and, my favourite, 'L'ape spaziale', a lurid mauve creation for ages eight and up and a cross between a praying mantis with amber wings and an American baseball player.

But the mist is clearing and I must get to work.

I sit under the arcade by the grand entrance to the Correr painting the impossible – San Marco across the Piazza – in the bitter cold. Although I am in the brightest sunlight, an arctic gale hurtles through the arches, blowing my paper and jostling my brushes on the ground. The intense winter light, flooding in from the Piazzetta, begins to hit the façade of San Marco just after ten o'clock (I had noticed this the day before). By twelve the effect will have gone so I have only under two hours of torment trying to capture the slow but constantly moving shadows. Suddenly the entire pearly façade is slatted with long rhythmical shadows cast by the serried rain-water spouts. This is exactly the effect I am aiming for and today the crisp shadows are more vivid than ever.

My teeth are chattering and my mittened fingers quivering with excitement and cold as I dash in the shadows. A sudden fiendish gust of wind scatters several vital brushes in all directions over the chequered marble floor. I scamper after them, retrieving them as they still roll. I resume: the shadows have slightly moved and, what is worse, look even better than before.

A lady comes up and asks politely what technique am I using? Is it tempera? No, it is not. A gentleman asks me the way to the nearest vaporetto stop. I am sorry but I do not know (actually it is just round the corner). Another elderly gentleman is extremely sorry to disturb me but he requires direction to a certain insurance agency. I say I do not know so he shows me a piece of paper with the address of the agency clearly written upon it and I say I am sorry but I really do not know. The old man is still reluctant to move but, thankfully, a lady in furs passes and says 'How beautiful' without looking, and the man teeters off. Soon there is another 'How beautiful' – this 'che bello!' seems to be the standard greeting to all artists, even very young children say it in a sing-song way, 'che bell'! che bell'!'

At the very height of my frenzy, patience and stamina exhausted, the inevitable happens and a noisy giggling party of unseasonable Benettons stop and gaggle round. They push and shove for a bit, some adjust their Walkmen whilst others nonchalantly chew gum. I wait for the inevitable question: 'Eenglish?'

I grunt.

Pause.

'You like Duran Duran?'

There is no answer to this.

Eventually they shuffle away shrugging. It is after twelve, shadow has drifted over the façade again. I am frozen and frustrated at not achieving the effect I was aiming at, and am finally left alone looking at the beauty of crystalline winter light with its long low shadows under a thin, palest milky blue sky. I give up, and go and have coffee.

One morning in late November, whilst Edmund was chomping through his egg and I was pretty much asleep, the sirens began to wail. I had never heard them before – there were two and they made a haunting duet. It meant the water in Venice was a certain amount (80 cms, I think) above sea level. Looking out of the grilled window over the canal we saw water already covering the Fondamenta and gently lapping up to the sill of the door of the trattoria opposite. The proprietor came out, looked at the water, made a theatrical gesture of resignation, went back inside and began to close up shop. The water continued to rise. When dressed, I was amazed to see the entrance hall outside our apartment under a foot or more of water. This was disconcerting. Rose, from upstairs, was standing on the bottom-most possible stair swivelling her early-Lucian Freud eyes, elegantly smoking a cigarette and staring at the water. 'Your friend Roderick telephoned and invited himself over for the weekend. He wants you to call him back. He sounded awfully nice,' she drawled. 'My friend Roderick is a middle-aged architect with a pig-tail, I'm afraid,' I said over the flood that separated us. ' I can't wait to meet him.' More swivelling of eyes. 'I'll bring you your waaaders . . .' She returned in her pencil-thin dress to the piano nobile and shortly came back with the waders. These were quite elaborate to lace on and came practically up to the top of your legs. You felt like a Cavalier.

The water continued to rise: high tide was at 11.30. I set off for the nearest public telephone. The first odd sensation was wading through the dark entrance hall, laboriously pushing open the front door against the weight of water and finding the calle outside even deeper in *acqua alta*; then slowly trudging through the heavy, clear water in the rain, your feet unable to leave the ground as if there was lead in your boots, the lumbering gait of a plodding, ungainly skater. At least, all the others in the street were doing the same slow haul, holding their umbrellas in one hand, their shoes and the shopping in the other, and very silly we all looked. I had never before realized how the levels of the pavement vary: sometimes a small campo could be completely above water, so for a moment you emerge to squelch like a duck on dry land only to plunge nearly up to your knees in the next alley. Narrow duckboards had been placed down the centre of the main shopping street, so there now was a continual procession of shoppers pacing

along, many in rather chic wellingtons, clutching colourful umbrellas. Although bizarre, everyone looked as if this was completely normal: they would step off the duckboard to buy vegetables, and stand around in groups chatting, unconcerned that they were up to their knees in water.

In a completely flooded restaurant a brooding waiter, bored, was placing inverted, dripping chairs on top of the tables. In a shop, an assistant was doing much the same to objects on the lower shelves. The first telephone I tried did not work, so I had to trudge into even deeper water near the Grand Canal. By the vaporetto stop of San Marcuola I stepped off a gang-plank into water which came halfway up my thighs, and finally got through to my pig-tailed friend, cocooned in Arts and Crafts suburban Chiswick, whilst here I was wearing great waders mid-thigh-deep in clear Venetian water, surrounded by floating plastic bottles, inexplicable drift-wood, and enormous soggy, empty, half-submerged cartons of washing powder. I heard a familiar voice. 'What? Speak up! Damned nonsense. Pull yourself together. Ridiculous place. See you on Saturday.'

It was from here, San Marcuola, that I took the vaporetto on the morning of the feast of the Salute, the 21st of November, when Venetians still give thanks for the liberation of Venice from a virulent plague in 1630. A clear and sparkling day: glittering water gently lapping over the ria; vaporetto down the Grand Canal and the many glass windows of the palaces would suddenly flash orange and gold as they caught the sun. This provided the mood of dazzling festivity, heightened by the sound of bells pealing at random over the whole city, but somehow intensifying as we approached the Salute. Crowds were hurrying over the votive bridge as we sailed under it, passing in front of the Salute itself.

The great portal of the church had been thrown open for this day only, and was swagged in crimson and gold on the patinated bronze, with a great festoon of laurel swinging above the heavy furled curtain of cardinal red. As the boat passed there was a brief glimpse of the interior radiating an intense white and gold. Just below the steps at the side, stalls had been set up selling apple dumplings – they smelt delicious mingling with the candles and the incense, and the sound of their frying added to the general jollity.

From all over Venice, crowds were flocking to the church. Smart children in colourful scarves clutching large balloons. At ten o'clock all the disparate bells turned to one tolling bell and the long procession of priests swayed two by two up the steps into the light, all chanting, their embroidered robes and lace flapping in the winter breeze, some wearing flat tweed caps, some berets, some so old that they had to be helped up the steps by their companions. The Bishop came last with a large gold mitre. Impassive at the very top of the stairs stood two guards in splendid Napoleonic uniform, huge black cloak half pulled back, black tricorn hats with enormous cockades of bright blue and red like colourful candy floss, they were leaning on swords and had two bold red stripes with brass buttons running up their trousers.

Stalls outside were laden with neat piles of clean white thick candles: people would buy them, carry them up the stairs and hand them over to waiting choirboys, their arms outstretched just inside the church. When each boy had amassed a heavy load – it only took a few minutes – he would pad away and be replaced by another. Inside the church all was crimson, crimson damask covered all the

usually bare columns, incandescent altar, a feeling of light, and celebration in the milling crowds. The icon over the altar had been decked out with an elaborate crown and necklaces, pink roses were placed between the long white candles, and the deep crimson hanging, draped from the corona above the altar, set the expressive, very white sculpture of the old woman of the banished plague into stark relief.

Outside, toasted almonds were being sold along with the apple dumplings, and it is this smell I shall always associate with the feast of the Salute.

I meet Carrie on the Zattere. She was sitting reading *The Europeans*, and we spread our picnic lunch on the white marble seat. Parma ham, salami and mortadella followed by rolls with green-veined Dolce Latte, very fresh Talèggio, blood-oranges, and I have bought two slices of Panforte, a sort of solidified candied peel with almonds and quite delicious. The bottle of bubbling acqua minerale makes a mauve shadow in the sun.

How familiar is the gentle rock and creak of the floating vaporetto stop as we wait for our number five boat, the *circolare sinistra*. We can see it approaching from the Sacca Fisola beyond the pink, crow-nested, gabled, dilapidated Stucky factory. Waiting with us in this very utilitarian grey shelter (how I long to redesign them in Venetian Gothic) are two jolly nuns chatting in Venetian dialect (which I still can never understand), and an old lady also in black sits clutching her shopping, calmly staring out at the water with eyes its exact shade of pale green. She has that noble thin aquiline face of a true Venetian. Has she ever left Venice in her long life, I wonder. Does she know the other world beyond the lagoon? The proprietress of a trattoria once told us that Venetians could all speak 'proper' Italian if they tried. She had never learnt the dialect herself, coming as she did from Jesolo where the dialect was considered common. She earnestly wanted to find out from Il barone Edmund the precise way to address Her Majesty the Queen in English. She was practising her 'Ma'am's as we left.

We sit out in the back of the boat almost on a level with its churning wake, loving the slosh and sparkling openness of the Giudecca. We get out by the Redentore and notice, close to, its delicate pencil-veining marble. Inside we find the caretaker hoovering, and he leads us to the sacristy, one of the most extraordinary rooms I have ever seen. Whilst he is trying to point out the conventional beauties of a dubious masterpiece hanging on the wall, we marvel at a whole collection of waxwork decapitated saints, rows of pale ecstatic heads under glinting glass domes. Their shiny eyes roll heavenwards as blood flows over bases lettered like old apothecary shops. San Fidelus a Sigmaringa has had his head gashed in half, and his brown cotton-wool hair and beard is given an eerie aureole by being lit from behind. The sacristan seems used to English reaction: he is tipped and we leave.

The boat journey soothes and San Giorgio Maggiore always astonishes. Carrie likens Gothic churches to barns and classical ones to drawing-rooms. How lucky we are to like both and how sad that Ruskin reserved his finest prose for vituperation. You enter a calm harmonious rational world which Palladio through his genius manages to make seem larger and more noble than the world outside. Beside being white it is also very clean and smells like a well-scrubbed boarding-house in North Wales. But, unlike the philosophy that created Colwyn Bay, this church has the most pleasing feeling of grandeur and dignity, and unlike a 'cosy' Nonconformist chapel is not in the least cold. The bold entasis of the clustered engaged pilasters, combined with the almost primitive, uncarved thick acanthus leaves of their capitals, give the whole church a solid, noble air. These unenriched capitals look like artichoke leaves and there are only two fluted columns with carved corinthian capitals, right by the altar. This is a perfect example of the moving power of classicism and its imagery. After enrichment by the altar, the great simple reveals of the thermal celestory windows give a satisfying feeling of depth, calm and solidity.

Always there is the feeling of water and its activity outside, which gives every building a sense of festivity.

In his book about Cardinal Consalvi, John Martin Robinson writes of the election of Pope Pius VII in Venice in 1800. It was occupied by the Austrians at the time, and Vienna was disappointed in the choice, so refused permission for the coronation to take place in San Marco. The Pope was therefore enthroned at San Giorgio and the overspill congregation sat outside in gondolas or filled the rooftops of the Piazza opposite, watching the ceremony through telescopes.

We ascend the campanile in a smooth lift manned by a monk. At the top we step into a blaze of light, bronze bells above us, and, beyond the smooth lagoon and above the strip of the Lido, the iridescent Adriatic, a pale manganese blue. I begin to hum the first movement of Tchaikovsky's fourth symphony which my scatty mind has just remembered from seeing the plaque on the Riva in the morning.

We have to change boats to go to the Lido. Quite by chance we see a friend's husband sketching on the quay. He sits on a folding stool wearing half-spectacles, puffing at a large briar pipe. We shout and wave from the boat, he looks up and graciously half-raises his hat as we chug by. The beauty of going to the Lido is the journey back. Even after only a day in Venice, it comes as a shock to see streets, trees and cars again, and large lit-up advertisements. It is still out of season and empty, which is what I like: the empty beach has a forlorn air and the ugly modern beach huts of the Grand Hotel des Bains look ridiculous. The hotel itself looks even more forbidding than usual, and the spirits of von Aschenbach, Diaghilev and Cole Porter do not rise. My favourite building is further down the front, the huge, mad, Moorish Grand Hotel Excelsior. It looks like a cross between the Brighton Pavilion, the Doges' Palace and the Alhambra. When we first knew it, it was cracked and covered in creeper, but now it is very smart indeed with all trace of character removed from the inside. I remember we dined there one Easter Day, the only couple in the vast dining room. Afterwards we walked through french windows directly out onto pale grey sand. Here a few Italian youths had started up a game of football. They were very stocky and bronzed, so the spirit of Diaghilev revived after all. On our way back we paused to admire the art nouveau tiles covering the whole of the neglected Anstonia Hotel. Next to the splendidly-named Villa Nelly we found a curious villa like something from the Vienna Secession. It would have looked more in place in Darmstadt.

The journey back gives you the best views of Venice, particularly in the early evening when the whole riva glows in a mysterious warm orange light which would look unspeakably vulgar if painted. This time we turn right and make the short but memorable journey through the Arsenale. Although I have never been to Wembley I feel it must have the same feeling of Empires passing by. Here a lone flimsy Chinese junk is moored, left over from the Regatta Storica, heightening this feeling of passing time. The last building is filled with a thousand bicycles. How exciting it is as we whoosh through the thin arch in the tall pale brickwork and out into the huge lagoon.

At the Fondamenta Nuove stop we stay on, and the boat continues to the cemetery island of San Michele. Had we been going to Torcello directly on one of the large two-tiered boats, we could have played our game of spotting the tomb of Frederick William Rolfe, which can just be glimpsed if you are quick, looking over the wall at the banks of stacked tombs like filing cabinets. But today we can only imagine it behind the pretty pink early nineteenth-century walls with their regularly spaced Gothic pavilions with mournful cypress trees pointing like green stalagmites. The gleaming white church is Coducci's earliest and in many ways his finest, with its delicate all-over rustication and curved pediment filled with a shell. The baptistery curves in like a barrel with a smooth melon dome on top. The old cloisters of the church are lined with worn tombs with bold neo-classical lettering. When we enter the main cemetery we are immediately compelled by the futuristic display of the modern tombs with their jagged, asymmetrical, highly polished marble, offset by chrome vases of plastic flowers and photographs of the deceased set in little ceramic ovals. All these have a gruesome fascination but, firmly not following the signs pointing to Ezra Pound, we go off in search of Stravinsky. We find someone has scattered at random a variegated bunch of carnations over the gravestone. Diaghilev's tomb is very strange with a menacing dome already slightly leaning.

To our great delight we discover a forgotten little room filled with the oddest urns. It has a neo-classical ceiling and is top-lit. As we slowly look round, savouring every monument, we can hear the sound of cicadas and cooing doves outside, the bright light casting strong shadows in this cool room. Out of one casket two bronze hands mysteriously rise, holding three dusty plastic flowers. Felicia de Rosa lies in her own little primitive hut like a Staffordshire Wesleyan chapel. Little Bruna Bergo (1920–1921) is contained in a baby pyramid. The photograph of Augusto Bortali Moretti shows a fine figure with a moustache wearing a Homburg. It is he who reminds us of the tube of toothpaste, and his casket has got a little amber opening in it to examine his ashes. They look exactly like delicious dried mushrooms. Perhaps the oddest monument is a cast-iron box supported by four webbed swan's feet. It resembles an old pedal sewing machine about to pad away.

On the next island, Murano, Carrie immediately finds a clear glass dachshund with three tiny baby dachshunds inside. She wants it but has to be deflected into looking for necklaces instead. The lovely, faded, old-fashioned ones are getting increasingly difficult to find, the ones with clusters of fruit, petals of pastel flowers, or simply a chain of oranges or lemons spaced with twisty tiny green leaves. We manage to find a beauty which Carrie immediately wears. She has forgotten the dachshund and luckily neither of us cares for pink flamingoes.

I love the chandelier shops, looking up to a world of writhing fantasy. Clear glass, iridescent or multi-coloured. We wanted to buy one as our wedding present but could never decide, and we have been looking ever since. Eventually, unknown to each other, we each found a perfect one in London, so now we have two. The Glass Museum has three extraordinary chandeliers in the main room, the furthest one with four huge columns that sprout at the base into surf and flying fish. Ravel would have loved the Giardino con fontana, a small formal glass garden with spun-glass fountain, around which birds and moths fly with spun-glass wings and the grass is made from ground particles of glass, blue, mauve and green. Another display is a very elegant clear glass cake-stand laid out with glass fruit, two glass pears, a glass apple, two glass tulips, and two parti-coloured feathery glass carnations.

We finally catch the double-decker boat to Torcello and watch our wake fan into the calm lagoon as the boat glides through the gently curving marked lane. The horizon blurs so you cannot tell sea from sky. This trip which usually induces reverie was once reduced to farce by Edmund deciding to paint a picture of it as we were travelling. He produced an enormously long, thin, irregularly shaped canvas which he unrolled as the journey unfurled. He would scowl at the horizon and begin rapidly to cover the canvas with grey, green and a touch of black. When a deserted island loomed he would dash it into the foreground and, as it passed, would stare at it over his shoulder saying, 'Archie, did you happen to notice the precise shade of pink on that wall?' Torcello arrived all too soon, and in his haste to pack up he spilt some yellow ochre on the back of the canvas. On disembarking, clutching stools, paints, easels and canvas whilst trying to smoke a cigarette, he laid the canvas face down on the herringbone brick path, leading to the Basilica. 'It's quite all right, Archie. It won't come off,' he said as he wiped the back with an old rag. When he picked it up it was seen that most of the paint had been left on the path, and the traces remaining on the canvas were embedded with grit and dirt.

Now we walk the brick path by the milky eau-de-nil canal overhung by tarmarisk which always reminds me of the most remote Scilly Isle, St. Agnes. A large party of school-girls has just entered the Basilica so we wait outside for them to leave. I do a quick sketch of Santa Fosca next door. You are struck at once inside the Basilica by its grave simplicity, the bare pink brick walls relieved by a subtle gold glinting from the mosaics at either end. The roof has plain wooden beams held up by grey columns. Hugh Honour says they are like moiré silk, and I agree. The capitals look to be fashioned of Burano lace.

The church is only lit from one side, the other a glowing echo of reflection. In the apse above the altar a solemn, even stern Madonna gazes down from a field of pale gold mosaic, the folds of her dress stylized in the Byzantine manner. Opposite her on the great west wall is the mosaic of the Last Judgement. This can be read like a cartoon, divided as it is into compartments. As usual, heaven seems a tame affair compared with all the frying of limbs in the bottom right-hand corner. There is a most beautiful frieze of petrified skulls on a black ground, with snakes writhing from their eyes.

Afterwards on the brick wall at the back of the church we watch a small lizard eat a large lumbering beetle, using the wall as a lever to force the beetle down. His snake-skinned sides are frantically panting with the effort. When the beetle is entirely inside, the lizard pauses for only a moment before darting off, looking no larger.

When we return across the lagoon, we see the Euganean Hills in sharp focus on our right, the summits covered in snow above the clouds, and the industrial suburbs smoking, their silhouettes like meccano toys in the foreground.

Carrie remarks that the main change in the streets of Venice in all the years we have been visiting is the recent rash of carnival

mask shops. They are everywhere, but mainly cluster around Rialto. It used to be difficult to buy reproductions of the original simple eighteenth-century masks, and it is still almost impossible, swamped as they are by modern psychedelic creations in fluorescent colours. Middle-aged ladies in tight black slacks can often be observed hand-crafting these masks in the shops. They have sour expressions as they recreate their youth, painting on particoloured butterflies. I feel the newly-revived Carnival in February must be a little ersatz also. I have seen enough art-photographs of fools in gold-lamé cloaks to prevent me ever wanting to witness them. It has a self-consciousness that does not appeal. The only time I saw the Regatta Storica it disappointed. Beside the races being over too fast, and the interminable pauses between them, the set pieces and fancy boats had the air of papier-mâché and brinylon fluttering in the breeze. Their occupants had the fixed grins of those in carnival floats. I prefer the full-bloodied vulgarity of the Easter Parade in New York, where the vision of a ten-storey-high inflated Olive Oyl doll slowly being hauled down Broadway is more telling.

Late afternoon light floods into the narrow calle. Worn vermilion bricks on either side glow, dotted with random blocks of stark white stone. Whilst stopping to admire this chance effect, a beaming priest pauses and asks us where we are from. He seems happy with our reply and he fumbles in his pockets and finds a thick wad of well-thumbed photographs. These are inscribed 'Il Papa in Inghilterra'. With glee he shows us every single photograph of the Pope in a dumpy white vehicle driving round Putney. The priest bubbles with enthusiasm and points out little details in each photograph we might have missed, and blesses us before continuing towards the sun down the calle. His clothes have that greenish tinge of old gravy that I remember from masters' gowns at school.

Nicholas and Roderick have arrived, both wearing long black coats: Nicholas like a highly strung whippet in an astrakhan collar, Roderick more a bulldog or genial buccaneer with bellowing voice and jaunty pig-tail. His interest in Abroad seems to be almost

confined to the exact influence a certain building has had on the design of Macclesfield Town Hall. We have all been working together on a scheme to create a painted neo-classical restaurant in London, so I want to show them the Caffè Pedrocchi in Padua, and some other places en route. We must look a rum trio as a car is hired in the Piazzale Roma. Usually I go by bus or train so it is a treat to be speeding so confidently through the interchanges of Mestre. We make a slight detour and stop to admire the Villa 'Malcontenta', which I have never seen before. It is taller than I expected, raised on a deep basement, and has very peculiar decorated chimneys. The front portico has a lovely green patina, and the back elevation is wonderful with its lunette window placed within a broken pediment, all with strong and inventive rustication. Unlike his followers in England, from the eighteenth century to his present revival, Palladio always managed to be completely inventive and all his villas, whilst recognizably using the same grammar in construction, manage to be different and unique. As we follow the banks of the Brenta, other villas are spotted, shuttered and forsaken in autumnal parks, between outposts of industrial development. Soon, they are thick on the ground, and we all comment on the richness of statuary and urnary on their parapets and pediments. Many are like elaborate chessmen. It is interesting to note that these are proscribed in Venice itself by the sumptuary laws, only the odd, telling obelisk being allowed to decorate the rooflines of palaces. This law has kept the skyline of buildings dignified, which might otherwise have become a distracting riot of enrichment.

The park wall of the Villa Pisani comes into view, pierced by gates giving tantalizing glimpses into a garden of mazes, vistas, belvederes and avenues. The front of the palace is enriched with Atlantes, and through the main door is immediately seen the long canal on an axis terminating in the famously theatrical stable block. Today I am astonished to see the snow of the Euganean Hills behind the stables, they look so close. My first visit to the Villa – twenty years ago – was haunting. We were the only visitors and the house was closed up. An elderly guide, however, offered to take us round and I can remember him creaking open the shutters in room after room, enfilade after enfilade, slanting floods of light advancing on the dark. The windows were broken, the fabrics torn, curtains hanging in tatters from faded gilt poles. Today all has changed and it has been beautifully restored inside and out. We are again the only visitors, and the easy-going guide does not seem to mind us exclaiming and photographing every new nuance of chalky marbling or colouring of the cornice. The beauty of the Villa is that it is an amalgam of several different styles, the original mid-eighteenth-century decorations, then the ravishing spacious Empire schemes created for Eugène de Beauharnais when he was Viceroy, then further into a variety of Italian Biedermeier uphol-stered in virulent green silks. I think it was here Hitler met Mussolini, but guide-books are vague on this point. There is an anteroom hung with engravings all the the many garden buildings.

The splendour of the Villa is the central Great Ballroom. The whole room is a satisfying harmony of ochres, ambers and grey and is dominated by Tiepolo's huge ceiling, the last he painted before leaving for Spain in 1762. I now understand that curious little notice which I read at the entrance whilst waiting for a guide, 'No lying down', because that is exactly what you do want to do in this ballroom. Lie down and lose yourself in this ceiling.

Afterwards we walk as if in a daze through the mud and fallen leaves of the empty park, its melancholy only broken by the sound of traffic on the busy road outside. A little headless statue in the undergrowth plays the bagpipes, and further on becomes a wistful duet when he is joined by another statue of a dwarf in a trilby plucking a mandolin. The belvedere bisects a long pergola and consists of an open dome supported by squinch arches. From the top of this belvedere you can practise your own Tiepolo compositions by putting your leg over the balcony and leaning out in theatrical attitudes. As we gaze at the reflection of the Villa through the water-lilies and dead leaves in the lake, a whole party of smartly-overcoated Japanese arrive and begin to photograph themselves in little tittering groups by the statues.

As we drive through Stra, Nicholas gets quite excited by Lorenzetti's decription of the nearby parks and gardens. 'Among the finest of these,' he reads, 'is the great SAONARA PARK with its plain white neoclassical villa which stands in the midst of the serene, smiling tranquillity of its great park; it seems to be almost isolated from the world by a curtain of green and silence. It was built in 1816, a year of great want, to help to relieve the local unemployment, by Antonio Cittadella-Vigodarzere from a design by the famous architect JAPELLI who was a specialist in designing parks and gardens. A quaint survival of the romantic taste of the times are the artificial GROTTOES planned with well devised effects of coloured lights and frightening shadows and constituting one of the attractions for which the villa is the resort of Venetians today, especially in the autumn.'

We try to find it, driving down culs-de-sac in modern housing estates, but alas it proves elusive. The reason for going to Padua, however, is to see the 'famous architect Japelli's' best-known work. Archie and I once stood outside the rather severely classical Caffè Pedrocchi and gasped at the same moment: I had noticed the

ground-glass hieroglyphics in the Egyptian room upstairs, and
Archie, looking into a shop window, had seen a pair of silk
stockings with lace round the top. Nicholas and Roderick do not
look in shop windows and I do not know what the other people in
the café can be thinking as we three stride in and begin crawling
under tables, photographing their legs, and all the details of the
Klismos chairs, eventually sitting down under the shiny Ionic
columns and having tea. As we leave the waiter says no, the bill has
already been paid. I am puzzled and the waiter explains it has been
paid by a young man who has been watching us. 'This is always
happening to me,' Roderick snorts as he storms out. Upstairs is a
most ingenious series of rooms demonstrating various styles,
centred on the white and gold concert hall, the Sala Rossini. Here
the band sits in a festooned draped balcony, large golden lyres
radiate in relief from the corners of the ceiling, and on the white

walls are frozen a swarm of glinting Napoleonic bees. Between this room and the loggia is the Sala Egiziana with sphinxes and stars on midnight-blue walls like Schinkel's stage-sets for *The Magic Flute*. All this is relieved by a spindly Gothic wing rather awkwardly tucked onto the side. Its balconies are based on the catherine wheels of the Palazzo Contarini-Fasan, and this troubadour style evokes the mood of Rossini's *Count Ory*.

Excited by so much neo-classicism, and refreshed by tea, we decide there is just time to drive into the hills to see the Temple of Canova and his birthplace at Possagno. This means we have to forgo the Giottos down the road, in the Cappella degli Scrovegni.

The country appears to be one mass of suburbia, light industrial estates and gardening centres but, approaching Monte del' Grappa, the landscape dramatically changes. Suburbia peters out, replaced by sublime snow-capped mountains. It is beginning to get dark as we began to switch-back up into the hills, and suddenly see the white glimmer of the votive temple half-way up the hillside in the distance. With its peristyle in front of a great shallow domed rotunda it resembles the Pantheon in Rome, only doric and grander. As we approach, a mist gathers in the twilight forming a vision of the spotlit temple above the mist with a back-drop of snow. It is the supreme fusion of the romantic and the classical. It is built out on a ramp of coloured pebbles laid in a diaper pattern, is extremely crisply detailed, and we are pleased to find the bold marble interior is all painted.

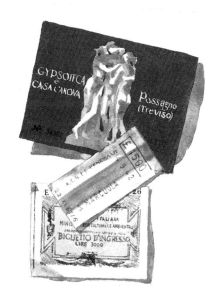

It lies on an axis with Canova's birthplace, where we have to pull on the bell for a long time to rouse the curator from his siesta. As usual, we are the only people here. Scarpa's very successful new extension wraps round the exterior of the 1830s Gypsoteca, showing that modern architecture can be sympathetic, and is filled with pleasing details like the tiny windows in the corners. All is white, white relieved only by the dark prongs laid into the surface of the plaster originals in order to make marble copies. It makes the statues look like prickly pears. The Gypsoteca is a very noble room indeed, top-lit through grand barrel vaults with shallow coffers. Everything including the walls has the colour and patina of ivory; apart from the white of the statues the only other colour comes from the rather jazzy maroon and ivory marble pattern of the floor.

The whole gallery is dominated by the prototype of a huge projected pyramid intended to commemorate Titian but finally used to house the sculptor's heart in the Frari. The rest of him lies with his step-brother in the temple up the hill. After all the lofty and expressive sculpture, it is a relief to enter the birthplace itself. Here, all is complete simplicity, a simplicity new to us, of late neo-classicism. All the mouldings, from skirting to cornice, are painted. Anterooms lined with banquettes are hung with Canova's Pompeian caprices painted over a black ground. In the birth-room itself hangs an extremely fine portrait of the sculptor by Sir Thomas Lawrence: it would be worth travelling so far to see this alone.

Back in Venice in spring we have cocktails on the Zattere, drinking Camparis and Negronis in the late afternoon light. The slatted floor built out over the water is scattered with the day's torn bills. A Russian liner passes slowly in the early twilight looking unattainably glamorous, its decks flushed warm with lights on the rigging. Faces stare at us, curious and alien. Who are they, and how have they been let out? My suggestion that we dine at the restaurant run by the lady I call Gina Lollobrigida's sister is vetoed. We decide where to dine and then sink back in silence, lost in the wonder of the thickening light.

One long summer we stayed at Montin's, just round the corner in San Trovaso. Above the restaurant with its garden at the back are a few simple rooms, and ours had a tiny balcony at the front where we would work, paint and read. For the whole summer just before dinner we would read Proust aloud, sipping wine. Once when we were buying some particularly cheap wine the man behind the counter pointed at it and in dumb show crossed his eyes whilst rapidly making circles round his ear with a pointed finger. That evening we found out what he had meant as we all passed out under its influence before the extract was finished. From then on we named the wine Venetian Blind.

Downstairs, the walls of the cosy cream and brown restaurant are packed with pictures hung frame to frame. The overall impression is pleasing and colourful, but must not be looked into too closely. There are pink table-cloths, the friendly waiters wear white jackets, and the menus reproduce some of the better paintings. Dinner for us here is almost a ritual. I always have antipasto Montin with shrimps, squid and mussels, tagliatelle al salmone, followed by either boiled tongue with salsa verde or fegato alla Veneziana with polenta. With this we drink elegant carafes of fizzy Prosecco or Pinot Bianco (della casa) and perhaps finish with tirimisu or the aptly-named zuppa inglese. They have recently installed a Grapparama, an ice drum containing all sorts of flavoured Grappa. We once had a tasting and decided they were all filthy: Edmund drank the lot. In summer the restaurant expands

into the three pergola tunnels in the garden at the back, but I prefer the out-of-season, more contained comfort at the front. We used to know the old proprietor behind the bar with his long aristocratic Venetian face. When all the customers had gone he would sit gambling at one of the tables, watching the Pope on television. His sallow portrait with dark hair now hangs on the back wall of the restaurant: it is a good likeness — although when we knew him his hair was white — and it is a Proustian shock to find his place behind the bar taken by his grandson who has the same face.

After dinner we might wander for a bit, return to the Piazza or go to a concert, certainly take a boat up and down the inky Grand Canal. On the night before the Reggata Storica in autumn there is a festival of lights on the Grand Canal. The bridges and borders are decorated with strings of paper lanterns. All motor-boats are banned. At ten in the evening a large floating platform roofed with a domed gazebo of coloured lights containing an orchestra playing Vivaldi proceeds slowly down the Canal, ending at San Marco. It is escorted by hundreds of little boats all lit with paper lanterns or flares and moving quietly on the dark water. The music is relayed by loudspeakers and in the interval we hear for the first time the mysterious lapping silence of old Venice, with boats creaking and people shouting across the water. Carrie is reminded of India, of candle-lit boats bobbing down-river at dusk in the holy city of Hardwar.

But tonight we make for La Fenice and, crossing the Grand Canal, look back at the Salute. It is lit up inside, and although spotlit seems to glow from within like burnished copper. I have only once seen an opera at the Fenice, *Il Trovatore*. Since then I have never been able to get tickets, but in spring and autumn there are series of concerts worth going to if only to see the most beautiful auditorium. We manage to get tickets for a concert performance of Ravel's *Daphnis et Chloë* — I wonder how Archie is going to express this in his peepshow — and sit in a box not quite under the roof this time, and are dazzled by the old rose, grey and gold of the interior. It is always such an excitement when the chandeliers slowly dim. It is a fine performance, the dawn music growing out of nothing, and well-sustained, but the girls in the next box *will* giggle at the wind machine. In the interval we walk the resplendent clear-cut foyers, stairs and concert rooms only slightly marred by the misintroduction of 'modern' art. They are palest grey and pinkish cream with lots of looking-glass and were built in the 1790s by Selva, who also designed the Canova Temple. He obviously had a fine eye for clean detail and elegance.

Afterwards, San Marco is irresistible. Now, in the dark, the arcades turn to flat stage scenery, and the tinsel façade of San Marco looks like a pavilion for a firework display. You feel it should at least be lit by flickering footlights. The café bands are in full swing, Florian's playing *Zampa*, Quadri's the tune from 'Amarcord', or perhaps the municipal wind band has set up and is doling out soupy versions of Verdi on a dozen clarinets.

The regular elaborate iron lamp-posts, with their bobbly-pink glass in the day, now give out a warm white light, which brings the architecture and carving into high relief, or plunges it into a soft velvety black. There is a bustle of people of all nationalities united in their enjoyment of this night.

We first met Colin on the last day of our honeymoon. Our waitress who had become very friendly as the weeks went by told us that a young Englishman had just arrived at the hotel and in order to make him feel at home but more especially as a treat for us she was going to sit him at our table. We were horrified and said no, no, but it was too late. He had already entered the room in a cream linen suit and was immediately charming and debonaire. We were glacially polite for only a moment before suddenly getting on so well. He was about to study art-history at Oriel, but more to the point he placed volume six of Proust on the table and I was reading only volume four. After dinner all three of us drank crême de menthe frappé at Florian's and madly sophisticated we felt. We were leaving the next day, he staying to hear Monteverdi: we talked with all the tripping easy pleasure of new friendship. Outside the bands played and Italian sailors sauntered by.

Today crême de menthe tastes to me like mouthwash and I

drank cognac. Carrie is mesmerised by the thin blue flame burning the last trace of alcohol from her drink. Tiny swirls of melting coffee beans begin to cloud her Sambuca.

One summer there was a weekly series of recitals at San Simeone Piccolo. We greatly looked forward to these, initially to see inside an otherwise inaccessible church, then, as the recitals were so good, to savour Chopin surrounded by architecture and, almost the best treat of all, to drift home down the entire length of the Grand Canal by night, the memory of the barcarolles still in our ears. We would have dinner outside in the little square in front of San Nicolò da Tolentino, watching its solemn columns grow shadowy and mysterious in the twilight. We would then wander round the corner to San Simeone for our after-dinner entertainment. The first time we entered the church it was draped in black for a Pope had just died. This made it dramatically grave and even the most impressive Polonaises sounded frivolous. By our next visit, a Venetian Pope had been declared and the church was grand and gay, hung almost entirely with luscious crimson damask. I like these moveable colour schemes, and it accorded perfectly with the jolly tinkling waltzes played on the sleek black piano. On the following visit, alas, the Pope had died again, and all was once more plunged into sublime gloom.

On the almost empty vaporetto afterwards we are able to sit right at the front, and are soon lost in beauty, lured by the lapping into the world of Chopin, of Fauré and perhaps tonight most of all of Offenbach whose barcarolle from *The Tales of Hoffmann* so perfectly sums up the mood of romantic, gently rocking opulence. We do not speak as we gaze at the glittering reflections in the indigo water lit by pink candelabra, cliffs of palaces drifting by, some floodlit, others dark but for their chandeliers. Just as their bottle-glass windows flashed gold and reflected the sun on the feast of the Salute, we now see beyond the glass to the many-tiered trees of Murano chandeliers ablaze within. The mood is so potent that it is not completely dispersed by a commercial flotilla of serenading gondolas passing slowly by. Here six or seven over-packed gondolas huddle round a central one bearing a bored man smoking a cigarette whilst playing a piano accordion, accompanying a tired old tenor in an old mackintosh singing inevitably 'O Sole Mio', a hideous tune that should never have left Naples.

The mood resumes as the convoy passes, lingers but for a moment and is utterly shattered at the next vaporetto stop. A party of English descend and jostle to the front of the boat, their loud braying voices strangling the loveliness:

'Hey! Don't push in front of Mummy!'

They settle down. I cannot look round, but have a vision of scrubbed healthy faces and sensible shoes.

'I say, have you done this before?'

'I should say so. But not by night.'

'Lovely isn't it?'

'Absolutely lovely.'

'It is absolutely lovely.'

'I say, isn't that the moon?'

'The moon, is it! How lovely.'

'It is the moon. Would you say it was a new moon?'

'It's practically a new moon.'

'It's practically almost a new moon, I'd say.'

'Gosh, a new moon in Venice, how lovely.'

'I say, isn't that the palace where I used to stay?'

'Couldn't say exactly. It might be.'

'They're awfully dark, you know. By day. I've never thought, well, you know, those pointed window things don't let the light in. Not very healthy really.'

'Hadn't thought about it.'

'You know, they're all built on piles.'

'Piles? Are they really? How very clever of them.'

'I say, isn't Harry a wonderful stepfather?'

'He's absolutely marvellous and, what's more, he absolutely loves it.'

'Isn't this our stop.'

'Is this our stop?'

It is. It is. Joy. Joy.

# BIZARRE DINOSAURS

# BIZARRE

Can you find this bizarre
dinosaur in the book?
(For answer, see page 32.)

# DINOSAURS

## SOME VERY STRANGE CREATURES AND WHY WE THINK THEY GOT THAT WAY

## CHRISTOPHER SLOAN

WITH A FOREWORD BY JAMES CLARK AND CATHY FORSTER

NATIONAL GEOGRAPHIC

WASHINGTON, D.C.

*To all the National Geographic staff, at the magazine, in television,
and in other divisions, as well as to the many talented artists and scientists
who helped bring these dinosaurs to life. —CS*

Founded in 1888, the National Geographic Society is one of the largest nonprofit scientific and educational organizations
in the world. It reaches more than 285 million people worldwide each month through its official journal, NATIONAL GEOGRAPHIC,
and its four other magazines; the National Geographic Channel; television documentaries; radio programs; films; books;
videos and DVDs; maps; and interactive media. National Geographic has funded more than 8,000 scientific research projects
and supports an education program combating geographic illiteracy.

For more information, please call
1-800-NGS LINE (647-5463) or write to the following address:
NATIONAL GEOGRAPHIC SOCIETY
1145 17th Street N.W., Washington, D.C. 20036-4688 U.S.A.

Visit us online at www.nationalgeographic.com/books
Librarians and teachers, visit us at www.ngchildrensbooks.org

For information about special discounts for bulk purchases, please contact
National Geographic Books Special Sales: ngspecsales@ngs.org.

For rights or permissions inquiries, please contact
National Geographic Books Subsidiary Rights: ngbookrights@ngs.org.

Library of Congress Cataloging-in-Publication Data available from the publisher on request.
Trade Hardcover ISBN 978-1-4263-0330-2
Reinforced Library Edition ISBN 978-1-4263-0331-9

Printed in China

# TABLE OF CONTENTS

This room is chock-a-block with fossils from
our expeditions with Chinese scientists
to western China. Careful study of these
fossils will give us a better picture of the
world of dinosaurs.

**DINOSAURS SEEM LIKE SOMETHING** from a fantasy world, but unlike unicorns, gryphons, and dragons, they actually existed. We know of them mostly from their bones, and there is nothing so exciting as watching the bones of a new dinosaur slowly take shape as they are extracted from their rocky grave. Paleontologists like us spend much of our lives digging for new fossils and then studying them to decipher the stories they hold. When a fossil is being excavated, our minds are racing: What kind of dinosaur is it? How much is preserved? Are there clues to how it died, what it ate, and how it moved? It is like assembling a jigsaw puzzle missing most of the pieces, and it's not always easy to see the whole picture. In this book you will find some surprising and baffling discoveries, dinosaurs with features nobody fully understands. We may never know everything we would like to know about them, but we can marvel at their strangeness. And who knows, perhaps one day you will grow up to be a paleontologist and discover even more bizarre dinosaurs. Or you might be the one to finally understand how some of their odd features were used.

**—JAMES CLARK AND CATHY FORSTER**

NAME
**AMARGASAURUS**
**(UH-MAR-GUH-SAWR-US)**

YEAR NAMED
**1991**

TYPE OF DINOSAUR
**SAUROPOD**

NORMAL ADULT SIZE
**33 FEET**

STOMPING GROUND
**PATAGONIA, ARGENTINA,**
**SOUTH AMERICA**

WHEN IT LIVED
**130 TO 125 MILLION**
**YEARS AGO**

ON THE MENU
**PLANTS**

*Amargasaurus's closest relative lived in what is now East Africa, but it didn't share its strange back fringe.*

8

# AMARGASAURUS
## HAD A FRINGED BACK.

**SEA MONSTERS** with fishlike fins on their backs come to mind when we try to imagine what *Amargasaurus* looked like. One finlike row would be bizarre enough, but the double row of spikes strung along *Amargasaurus's* back pushes it to extremes. Why the fringe? It would have been useless for defense, but it could have been attractive to mates. But maybe we're interpreting the spines incorrectly. Perhaps instead of a double fringe, the two rows of back spines supported a mass of flesh. A thick, deep neck might have helped protect *Amargasaurus* by making the animal look too big for some predators to eat.

Scientists discovered a fairly complete skeleton of *Amargasaurus* in Argentina.

9

# CARNOTAURUS
## HAD BULL HORNS.

**CARNOTAURUS** was a distant relative of *Tyrannosaurus rex*, and its tiny arms give it a *T. rex* look. Yet *Carnotaurus* had small teeth for a big meat-eating hunter. It also had a pair of stubby, chunky horns jutting out from its brow like a bull. Brow horns like these are mostly seen among ceratopsids—plant-eating dinosaurs, not meat-eaters. Ceratopsids may have used their horns for defense, for competing with rivals, or for attracting mates. It is possible that *Carnotaurus* was a scavenger, rather than a big hunter, and used its horns in the same ways, but between meaty meals.

*Carnotaurus's* name, meaning "meat-bull," links its bull-like horns to its meat-eating habits.

The almost complete fossil of *Carnotaurus* had horns and skin impressions that showed it had bumps along its back.

NAME
*CARNOTAURUS*
(KAR-NO-TAWR-US)
. . . . . . . . . . . . . . . . .

YEAR NAMED
1985
. . . . . . . . . . . . . . . . .

TYPE OF DINOSAUR
THEROPOD
. . . . . . . . . . . . . . . . .

NORMAL ADULT SIZE
30 FEET
. . . . . . . . . . . . . . . . .

STOMPING GROUND
PATAGONIA, ARGENTINA,
SOUTH AMERICA
. . . . . . . . . . . . . . . . .

WHEN IT LIVED
83 to 65 MILLION
YEARS AGO
. . . . . . . . . . . . . . . . .

ON THE MENU
MEAT

Stegosaurs such as
*Tuojiangosaurus* had many styles
of armor. But their body shape
was almost always the same, a
small head with a tanklike body.

EXPERT KNOWLEDGE

NAME
*TUOJIANGOSAURUS*
(TWHOA-JEE-ANG-OH-SAWR-US)

YEAR NAMED
1977

TYPE OF DINOSAUR
STEGOSAUR

NORMAL ADULT SIZE
23 FEET

STOMPING GROUND
SICHUAN, CHINA, ASIA

WHEN IT LIVED
161 to 155 MILLION
YEARS AGO

ON THE MENU
PLANTS

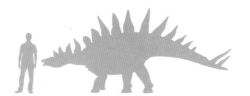

# TUOJIANGOSAURUS
## HAD SPIKED SHOULDERS.

**MANY STEGOSAURS** have fierce-looking tail spikes and what look like flat stones sticking out of their backs. These are fancy forms of osteoderms, bony plates that some animals, such as dinosaurs and crocodiles, wear in their skin. *Tuojiangosaurus* added one more weapon to its armor—shoulder spikes that jut out from its shoulders. It is possible that all of this scary gear was only used to look impressive to mates, but it must also have made *Tuojiangosaurus* look a little less tasty to predators.

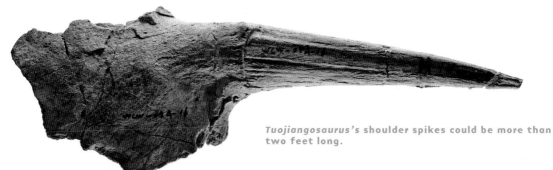

*Tuojiangosaurus's shoulder spikes could be more than two feet long.*

13

# NIGERSAURUS
## HAD A VERY WIDE MOUTH.

**NO OTHER ANIMAL—EXTINCT OR ALIVE—HAS A MUZZLE** quite like *Nigersaurus*. Other long-necked sauropods had narrow snouts with peglike teeth, nothing like *Nigersaurus's* wide mouth with comblike rows of tiny teeth. Behind each toothy row in *Nigersaurus's* skull sit as many as eight other sets of teeth—that's around 500 spare teeth standing ready to replace worn ones. *Nigersaurus* held its head at a sharp angle to its neck, causing its mouth to be pointed toward the ground. This dinosaur was found in the Sahara desert, which in its time was a wet, plant-rich environment. Its unusual mouth was probably useful for constantly mowing soft plants.

*Nigersaurus's* thin skull bones lead scientists to think it may not have been able to eat much more than soft plants.

14

Many fossils of medium-sized *Nigersaurus* have been found in Niger. Its name means "Niger lizard."

NAME
*NIGERSAURUS*
*(NEE-ZHERE-SAWR-US)*

YEAR NAMED
1999

TYPE OF DINOSAUR
SAUROPOD

NORMAL ADULT SIZE
30 FEET

STOMPING GROUND
SAHARA DESERT, NIGER,
AFRICA

WHEN IT LIVED
110 MILLION
YEARS AGO

ON THE MENU
PLANTS

15

*Masiakasaurus* looked very fierce, but it had to watch out for the larger meat-eating dinosaurs and the many kinds of crocodiles living around it in Madagascar.

EXPERT KNOWLEDGE

NAME
*MASIAKASAURUS*
(MUH-SHEE-KUH-SAWR-US)

YEAR NAMED
2001

TYPE OF DINOSAUR
THEROPOD

NORMAL ADULT SIZE
7 FEET

STOMPING GROUND
MAHAJUNGA, MADAGASCAR, AFRICA

WHEN IT LIVED
70 TO 65 MILLION YEARS AGO

ON THE MENU
MEAT

# MASIAKASAURUS
## HAD A NASTY BITE.

**THE CHAMPION OF BIZARRE TEETH** is *Masiakasaurus,* meaning "vicious lizard." This collie-sized dinosaur from Madagascar was a meat-eater, but exactly how it hunted we don't know because no living animal has teeth like this. In the back of its mouth, *Masiakasaurus's* teeth were shaped like knives with serrated edges, but toward the front they were cone-shaped, curved, and pointed nearly straight ahead. Knifelike teeth are good for slicing, so maybe *Masiakasaurus* opened its mouth wide and sliced larger prey with its back teeth. The hooked front teeth may have been used for stabbing or snagging small mammals, lizards, or birds.

The front part of *Masiakasaurus's* lower jaw shows a couple of curved teeth.

*Deinocheirus's long arms may have been attached to a 40-foot body.*

# DEINOCHEIRUS
# HAD LONG, CLAWED ARMS.

IF EVER THERE WAS A DINOSAUR MYSTERY, it is Mongolia's *Deinocheirus*, meaning "terrible hand." Only its arms and a few other bits have ever been found. But what arms! Each one is eight feet long with three ten-inch claws at the end. No one really knows what *Deinocheirus* was. Perhaps it had the long neck, legs, and tail of an ornithomimosaur, and its plant-eating habits as well. But to work with these arms, its body would have been enormous, as big as a *T. rex.*

NAME
*DEINOCHEIRUS*
(DYE-NO-KAI-RUS)

YEAR NAMED
1970

TYPE OF DINOSAUR
THEROPOD

NORMAL ADULT SIZE
UP TO 40 FEET

STOMPING GROUND
GOBI DESERT OF MONGOLIA,
ASIA

WHEN IT LIVED
70 MILLION
YEARS AGO

ON THE MENU
PROBABLY PLANTS

Nobody knows how feathery
*Deinocheirus* might have been.
Large dinosaurs would have had
fewer feathers than small ones
because larger animals need to
lose body heat, not keep it.

19

*Dracorex* was a pachycephalosaur, meaning "thick-headed lizard."

NAME
**DRACOREX
(DRA-KOHR-EX)**
. . . . . . . . . . . . . . . . . .

YEAR NAMED
**2006**
. . . . . . . . . . . . . . . . . .

TYPE OF DINOSAUR
**PACHYCEPHALOSAUR**
. . . . . . . . . . . . . . . . . .

NORMAL ADULT SIZE
**10 FEET**
. . . . . . . . . . . . . . . . . .

STOMPING GROUND
**SOUTH DAKOTA, U.S.A.,
NORTH AMERICA**
. . . . . . . . . . . . . . . . . .

WHEN IT LIVED
**67 to 65 MILLION
YEARS AGO**
. . . . . . . . . . . . . . . . . .

ON THE MENU
**PLANTS**

# DRACOREX
## HAD A VERY BUMPY HEAD.

**THE SPIKY SKULL OF THIS DINOSAUR** is so nasty looking it was named *Dracorex hogwartsia,* meaning "dragon king of Hogwarts," for the wizardry school of the Harry Potter books. But this creature was not as fierce as it appears. It is a plant-eating pachycephalosaur. Others of this group sport helmetlike bony domes on their heads. It may be that they used their thick skulls to butt each other, the way rams and goats do today. Some scientists think *Dracorex* isn't a separate creature at all, but a young pachycephalosaur that hasn't grown its dome yet.

This fossil skull of *Dracorex* was found in the famous fossil formation known as Hell Creek, in South Dakota.

21

# PARASAUROLOPHUS
## HAD A MUSICAL HEAD.

**PARASAUROLOPHUS HAD THE MOST BIZARRE HEADGEAR** of any of the duckbill dinosaurs—and the most puzzling. When *Parasaurolophus* breathed through its nose, air would pass through a doubled-back tube inside the long crest. Was it for a super sense of smell? To warm the air? Just for show? Scientists made a model to see what sound the tube would make if air passed through it. They discovered that *Parasaurolophus's* crest could make wonderful hornlike sounds. It may have used these sounds to communicate with others.

22

These duckbilled hadrosaurs are known for their bill-like mouth and crest, but the inside of their mouth is bizarre as well. They have thousands of teeth.

NAME
*PARASAUROLOPHUS*
(PARE-UH-SAWR-ALL-UH-FUSS)

YEAR NAMED
1922

TYPE OF DINOSAUR
HADROSAUR

NORMAL ADULT SIZE
31 FEET

STOMPING GROUND
ALBERTA, CANADA, AND NEW MEXICO, U.S.A., NORTH AMERICA

WHEN IT LIVED
76 MILLION YEARS AGO

ON THE MENU
PLANTS

23

EXPERT KNOWLEDGE

**NAME**
*STYRACOSAURUS*
*(STY-RACK-OH-SAWR-US)*
. . . . . . . . . . . . . . .
**YEAR NAMED**
1913
. . . . . . . . . . . . . . .
**TYPE OF DINOSAUR**
CERATOPSID
. . . . . . . . . . . . . . .
**NORMAL ADULT SIZE**
18 FEET
. . . . . . . . . . . . . . .
**STOMPING GROUND**
ALBERTA, CANADA,
NORTH AMERICA
. . . . . . . . . . . . . . .
**WHEN IT LIVED**
75 MILLION
YEARS AGO
. . . . . . . . . . . . . . .
**ON THE MENU**
PLANTS

Horned dinosaurs with frills
appear to have got their start
in Asia, but most of the large
ones with elaborate head
armor, such as *Styraco-
saurus*, have been found in
North America.

# STYRACOSAURUS HAD A HUGE SPIKED COLLAR.

**THE SHARP SPIKES** on *Styracosaurus's* neck frill look dangerous, but these animals weren't predators. And the spikes probably added no more protection than the less-spiky frills of other ceratopsid dinosaurs. A large meat-eater, such as *Albertosaurus*, could easily have chomped on *Styracosaurus's* unprotected hindquarters. It may be that the main purpose of the armor was not offense *or* defense. It is just as likely that the big frills were used to show off and attract mates. The earliest known member of this group, *Yinlong*, was found in 2004 in western China. Knobs on the back of its skull show that horned dinosaurs were close relatives of the pachycephalosaurs.

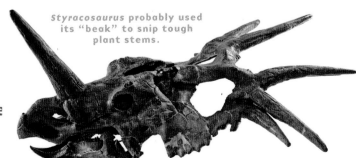

*Styracosaurus* probably used its "beak" to snip tough plant stems.

25

# EPIDENDROSAURUS
## HAD A SUPER-LONG FINGER.

**THE AYE-AYE,** a bizarre lemur from Madagascar, has one extra-long finger on each hand that it uses to fish tasty bugs out of holes in tree bark. That

LONG THIRD FINGER →

← HIND FOOT

*Epidendrosaurus's* long finger was preserved as an impression on this flat stone.

may be what tiny *Epidendrosaurus* was doing with its super-long finger as well. Its sharp, curved claws also suggest that this Chinese dinosaur, like the aye-aye, scampered around in trees. A close relative of the earliest birds, *Epidendrosaurus* was likely covered in a feathery coat. Yet unlike *Microraptor*, another tiny, feathered theropod, there is no evidence *Epidendrosaurus* flew.

NAME
*EPIDENDROSAURUS*
(EHP-IH-DEN-DROH-SAWR-US)

YEAR NAMED
**2002**

TYPE OF DINOSAUR
**THEROPOD**

NORMAL ADULT SIZE
**LESS THAN ONE FOOT**

STOMPING GROUND
**GOBI DESERT OF CHINA, ASIA**

WHEN IT LIVED
**160 MILLION
YEARS AGO**

ON THE MENU
**SMALL MAMMALS, INSECTS**

*Epidendrosaurus*'s third finger is almost twice as long
as its other fingers.

27

NAME
*GIGANTORAPTOR*
(JAI-GAN-TOH-RAP-TUR) . . . . . . . . . . .

YEAR NAMED
2007 . . . . . . . . . . . . . . . . . . . . . . . . . . . . . . . . .

TYPE OF DINOSAUR
THEROPOD . . . . . . . . . . . . . . . . . . . . . . . . . .

NORMAL ADULT SIZE
26 FEET . . . . . . . . . . . . . . . . . . . . . . . . . . . . . .

STOMPING GROUND
GOBI DESERT OF CHINA, ASIA . . . . . .

WHEN IT LIVED
85 MILLION
YEARS AGO . . . . . . . . . . . . . . . . . . . . . . . . . .

ON THE MENU
PROBABLY MEAT

Other fossilized oviraptorids have been found
sitting on clutches of eggs like nesting birds.
It is possible that *Gigantoraptor* did the same.

# GIGANTORAPTOR
## HAD A GIANT BEAK.

**NO ONE EXPECTED ANYTHING LIKE GIGANTORAPTOR,** a giant birdlike dinosaur, to ever be found. Yet that's what happened in 2005. Weighing in at an estimated 3,000 pounds, *Gigantoraptor* is many times bigger than other oviraptorids, which are the size of ostriches or smaller. What surprised scientists most is that they thought dinosaurs became smaller as they became more birdlike. But *Gigantoraptor* upsets that idea. This dinosaur was probably a meat-eater like other theropods, but it is possible that it ate plants as its much smaller cousin *Caudipteryx* did. *Gigantoraptor* might have had feathers like *Caudipteryx*, too, but how feathery it was, no one knows. It probably looked like a giant parrot with a bony tail, with at least some feathers and a big toothless beak.

**PARALITITAN** was among the largest of the sauropods. It weighed at least 40 tons, about the same as eight pickup trucks.

**SPINOSAURUS** is best known for the six-foot-long spines that may have made a sail or a hump on its back.

**AFROVENATOR**, whose name means "African hunter," may have been a distant relative of *Spinosaurus*.

**CARCHARODONTOSAURUS** Named "shark-toothed dinosaur," *Carcharodontosaurus* was among the largest known meat-eaters.

**NIGERSAURUS**

**MAJUNGASAURUS** was the biggest meat-eater in Madagascar, which broke off from Gondwana and grew its own dinosaurs for millions of years.

**AMARGASAURUS**

**MASIAKASAURUS**

**LEAELLYNASAURA** was from the very far south of Gondwana. It might have had eyes that could see well during cold, dark winter months.

**CARNOTAURUS**

# GONDWANA
## THE SOUTHERN HEMISPHERE

**BIZARRE DINOSAURS** didn't live alone. They lived with many other dinosaurs, as well as other animals and plenty of plants. They lived in many places around the world, over millions of years. For much of the time dinosaurs ruled the Earth, there were only two continents. These continents were so big we call them supercontinents. The one in the southern hemisphere is called Gondwana. On this page is a selection of typical Gondwanan dinosaurs, a mix of some of the dinosaurs you met earlier in the book and some others you might already know.

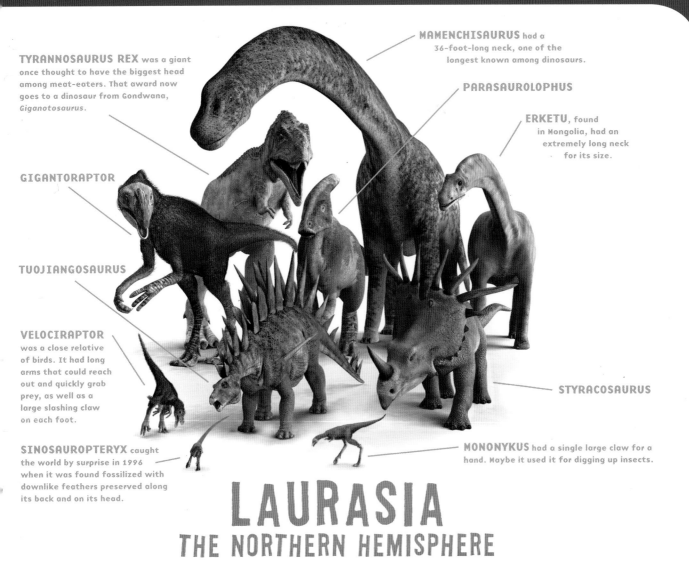

**TYRANNOSAURUS REX** was a giant once thought to have the biggest head among meat-eaters. That award now goes to a dinosaur from Gondwana, *Giganotosaurus*.

**MAMENCHISAURUS** had a 36-foot-long neck, one of the longest known among dinosaurs.

**PARASAUROLOPHUS**

**ERKETU**, found in Mongolia, had an extremely long neck for its size.

**GIGANTORAPTOR**

**TUOJIANGOSAURUS**

**VELOCIRAPTOR** was a close relative of birds. It had long arms that could reach out and quickly grab prey, as well as a large slashing claw on each foot.

**STYRACOSAURUS**

**SINOSAUROPTERYX** caught the world by surprise in 1996 when it was found fossilized with downlike feathers preserved along its back and on its head.

**MONONYKUS** had a single large claw for a hand. Maybe it used it for digging up insects.

# LAURASIA
## THE NORTHERN HEMISPHERE

**THE SUPERCONTINENT** of Laurasia was separated from Gondwana long enough for the dinosaurs in the two hemispheres to become quite different. On this page is a group of Laurasian dinosaurs, again a mix of those you met earlier and some you might know already. By the end of the Mesozoic era (dinosaur times), sauropods such as *Paralititan* were the main plant-eaters in Gondwana, while in Laurasia it was dinosaurs like *Styracosaurus* and *Parasaurolophus*. The meat-eaters in Gondwana were mostly abelisaurs such as *Carnotaurus*, and those in Laurasia were coelurosaurs such as *T. rex*.

## GLOSSARY

**ABELISAUR:** A group of meat-eaters that lived mostly on the Southern Hemisphere supercontinent of Gondwana.

**CERATOPSID:** One of five groups of bird-hipped, or ornithischian, dinosaurs. Ceratopsids walked on all fours and had horns and elaborate bony frills.

**CAUDIPTERYX:** A small Chinese beaked theropod found fossilized with small stones in its gut to help it digest plants.

**COELUROSAUR:** A member of Coelurosauria, a group of theropods closely related to, and including, birds.

**HADROSAUR:** A member of a group of bird-hipped, or ornithischian, dinosaurs. Hadrosaurs walked on four legs much of the time, had bill-like mouths, and are called "duckbills."

**MESOZOIC:** A geological era that lasted from 251 to 65 million years ago. It is often called the Age of Dinosaurs since they were the dominant land animal of that time. It is broken into three main periods, the Triassic (251 to 199 million years ago), the Jurassic (199 to 145 million years ago), and the Cretaceous (145 to 65 million years ago).

**ORNITHOMIMOSAUR:** A group of theropods, most of which were toothless and had horny beaks. Their appearance was ostrich-like, earning them their name, which means "bird-mimic lizard."

**OVIRAPTORID:** A birdlike theropod with a shortened snout and a beaklike, toothless mouth.

**PACHYCEPHALOSAUR:** A member of Pachycephalosauria, one of five groups of bird-hipped, or ornithischian, dinosaurs. They walked on two legs and had large bony domes on their skulls.

**PREDATOR:** An animal that lives by preying on others.

**SAUROPOD:** A member of Sauropoda, one of the two main branches of the lizard-hipped, or saurischian, dinosaurs. They walked on four legs and had long necks and large bodies.

**SCAVENGER:** An animal that feeds on animals that are already dead.

**STEGOSAUR:** A member of Stegosauria, one of five groups of bird-hipped, or ornithischian, dinosaurs. Stegosaurs walked on four legs and had small heads and large tank-like bodies with armored plates and spikes.

**THEROPOD:** A member of Theropoda, one of the two main branches of the lizard-hipped, or saurischian, dinosaurs. They had three toes, walked upright on two legs, and most were meat-eaters.

## CREDITS

The realistic color illustrations in this book are computer-generated models that took many people to create. The project was led by the Art Department at National Geographic Magazine. The base models for all of the dinosaurs were prepared by 422 South. All of the photography is by Ira Block, unless otherwise noted.

*Amargasaurus:* Art by Renegade 9. Photographed at Museo Argentino de Ciencias Naturales (MACN), Buenos Aires.
*Carnotaurus:* Art by Pixeldust Studios. Photographed at MACN.
*Tuojiangosaurus:* Art By Pixeldust Studios. Photographed at the Institute of Vertebrate Paleontology and Paleoanthropology (IVPP), Beijing.
*Nigersaurus*: Art by Pixeldust studios. Photo © M. Hettwer, courtesy of Project Exploration.
*Masiakasaurus:* Art by Pixeldust Studios. Fossil from the collection of the Université d'Antananarivo, Madagascar.
*Deinocheirus:* Art by Pixeldust Studios. Fossil from the collection of the Mongolian Academy of Sciences.
*Dracorex:* Art by DamnFX. Photographed at the Children's Museum of Indianapolis.
*Parasaurolophus:* Art by Pixeldust Studios. Photograph taken at the Royal Ontario Museum (ROM), Toronto.
*Styracosaurus:* Art by Renegade 9. Photographed at ROM, Toronto.
*Epidendrosaurus:* Art by Pixeldust Studios. Photographed at IVPP, Beijing.
*Gigantoraptor:* Art by Pixeldust Studios.
**Pages 30-31:** Art by Pixeldust Studios.

**Answer to question on title page:** Tuojiangosaurus